Wildlife of
Galveston

To Karol –
Welcome to my
world !

Jim Stevenson

by Jim Stevenson

VanJus Press
Galveston

Photographs
Jim Stevenson
(eight photographs by Alan Murphy and
Brian Small)

Cover Design and Layout
Justine Gilcrease

For information about the Galveston Bird
Club contact Jim Stevenson at (409)
737-4081 or snakeman@phoenix.net

ISBN 0-9666438-1-X

Dedication:
To all those whose eye is on the sparrow.

Acknowledgment

I would like to express my deepest appreciation to the Gilcrease family, without whose help this book would not have been possible.

I should also express my gratitude to Alan Murphy and Brian Small for unselfishly sharing several photographs to complete the bird plates.

Contents

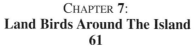

CHAPTER **1: The Lure of Galveston:
Personal Notes**

My earliest recollections of Galveston take me back to my late ornithologist father speaking of it with regard to its spring bird migration. He spoke of the vast numbers of songbirds that struggled to reach its shores and decorated the bushes with color like so many Christmas ornaments. Even at an early age, a little junior birder, I dreamed of Galveston and promised myself that I would one day experience the rush of dozens of species of multicolored feathered gems, flitting about on a lovely spring afternoon.

In preparation for my master's thesis many years later at Florida State, I conducted research on bird migration for Dr. Francis James, who had taken my father's place at FSU upon his early retirement. My work had been entirely in Florida, but Fran suggested I locate a research plot on the western Gulf similar to my study site on the Florida coast. Like a neon beacon from the past, the name "Galveston" flashed before my eyes and away I went!

After the lengthy drive from my beloved Tallahassee, I cut down Highway 124 and found myself on stark Bolivar Peninsula–a pretty desolate place back in the mid-70's. The excitement of the Upper Texas Coast quickly began, as elegant Scissor-tailed Flycatchers lined the phone wires. My adrenalin raced as species after species of unfamiliar birds appeared before me as if in a dream. Mottled Ducks. A frigatebird. And a Burrowing Owl where, sadly, they can no longer be found today. Even before arriving in Galveston (which I didn't even know was an island at the time), my avian taste buds were dripping with great birds. Oh my, a flock of Roseate Spoonbills!

The ferry ride across was agonizingly slow, but the terns, gulls and pelicans distracted me from the anxiety of being so close to my boyhood enchantment. Then finally, I drove onto the fabled land of avian plenty, and simply followed the traffic, not knowing where I was or where I was going. I found myself on the mighty seawall, forever a symbol and monument to the island's resilience and courage. West I went, intrigued by the businesses, warmly drawn to the water below, and not completely ignoring the young ladies strolling along the seawall on this rather warm day. I was here–where were the birds?

Words cannot adequately describe the sensations that I experienced as Seawall became FM 3005 and I returned to the more natural habitat of west Galveston Island. Joining the ducks, spoonbills and flycatchers already mentioned were White-faced Ibis, a marvelous caracara, and a flock of splendid Black-necked Stilts. But while still almost on "excitement overload," the unmistakable form of a male Scarlet Tanager zipped past my truck and I watched it disappear into a small plot of oak trees on the late Dr. Abe Levy's property. He became my first friend on Galveston, and his love for birds– and his dear wife–always warmed my heart. They have joined my father now in the great bird watch in the sky, but I'll never forget his face when I gave him a picture I took of the Scarlet Tanager in his yard so many years ago.

The Bolivar F

The Mighty Seawall

Shortly, I continued my search for "just the place" as I slowly drove out Old Stewart Road west.The wonderful forest which is now the Laffite's Cove Nature Preserve (heretofore called "the Preserve") was too big to serve as a parallel study site to my Florida plot. I then began feeling pessimistic upon returning to 3005, as the open grassland of the State Park and cow pastures just weren't the habitat I required for my graduate work. But past Jamaica Beach, a little way beyond my dear friends Jerry and Becky Smith's bait shop, I spotted a tiny isolated forest from the road. Taking some neighborhood streets to the base of it, I stepped out of my truck and strolled up to the woods for my first experience with my future home. Indigo Buntings darted around the bushes like unnatural turquoise splotches in nature's panorama, and hummingbirds zigged and zagged through the honeysuckle almost as fast as my heartbeat. It would have been impossible to know at the time, but I had come home.

After finding eleven species of warblers and many other migrants within the forest, there was little doubt that this was to be my study area. It was a mound of dirt piled up like a butte, about the size of a football field, with the soil taken from the west side of the road where the resultant lake now rests. Around the top stood the old corral fence that conveyed the property's purpose: A cattle pen for hurricanes–about fourteen feet above sea level. What a unique and mysterious place I had found!

Over the following years, during which I completed a master's thesis and fifteen years of teaching zoology, marine biology and ecology to college-bound bio majors, I returned to this site often. Frequently, my students and I camped behind the cover of its trees on the flat interior of the woods, and had worlds of fun birding and learning, as the island gave up her secrets. It

My beloved Heartbreak Hammock

was on one of these trips this oasis received its name. While off birding, some of our equipment was stolen, and we were crushed to discover the deed upon our return. We named the location "Heartbreak Hammock," and, although some objected, the name will stick, in honor of my former students and friends.

In 1996, in a winter filled with tragedy, my life was mired in deep depression from indescribable personal loss, and the thought of living out my life in Tallahassee seemed a poor prospect. On spring break, I journeyed out to Heartbreak Hammock, to try to put the pieces of my life back together. In a discovery that seemed to drive the proverbial stake through the heart, I found "no trespassing" signs blocking my entrance to historical paradise.

But, as I have always believed that windows open when doors shut, I went to visit the owner of the property, who was an excellent contractor, for permission to bird watch on my Mecca. He kindly granted that permission, and the next words out of his mouth dictated the direction of the rest of my life. *"You know, I've been thinking about selling that property."* Suddenly, I understood all that had happened to me, and my future suddenly seemed to sparkle.

Within an hour, I had drawn up a design for my house–brown with a green roof–to be placed unobtrusively in the middle of the forest, without removing so much as a limb. Because the owner was a contractor, the whole thing was quickly a done deal. There was a subtle irony, however, at the fact that the "no trespassing" signs were placed there because some kids had apparently been camping in there a few times in the past. Hmmm.

I sold two houses in Tallahassee, took an early retirement, tied up other loose ends, and returned to Galveston in August to stay. Since then I have founded bird clubs, along with teaching college classes and doing consultant work. But my greatest joy is writing bird articles for newspapers while sitting behind the thirty feet of glass that overlooks my pond, fruiting trees, and myriads of birds. On bad days–which are few–I prop up my feet on my father's old desk and remind myself that heartbreaks may eventually be followed by heartfelt joy, and that windows open when doors slam shut. And survivors of life's hurricanes can find joy amongst the wildlife and beauty of Galveston Island.

So it seems to be with my new Texas neighbors. As the beauty and pace of life on a barrier island brings reduced stress and appreciation for simple things, folks I know are strangely tied to the island's natural resources. To Becky Smith, it's a long

Jim identifying a spring migrant

Galveston beach complete with sargasso weed

gaze out her store's upstairs window at a flock of her "Sandies" (Sandhill Cranes). Patrick McGuffy would tell of sitting for hours in Apfell Park doing nothing but watching for Clapper Rails. And for countless people, a walk through the Preserve with binoculars in tow is an avian dream come true.

But Galveston is far more than just a good birding area (OK, a GREAT birding area!). Just ask the folks who bring their families for a day of fishing, swimming and beachcombing down at San Luis Pass. Or ask any of thousands of Houston families who stay along the seawall and spend weekends splashing in the water and frying in the intense sun. There is something special about Galveston Island, and the whole is greater than the sum of its examples. Wilderness, shorelines, monster oak trees, birds everywhere, great fishing, and the unique seawall; all are only part of a greater mosaic that excites visitors and refreshes residents. What a place to call home!

CHAPTER 2: Galveston Island as an Ecosystem

Barrier islands such as ours are natural results of the geological actions of rivers, erosion, ice ages and a host of other forces of nature. These elegant geophysical formations extend along the upper gulf coast from Dog Island (south of my hometown of Tallahassee, Florida) to Galveston. Others extend down the central and south Texas coastline almost to Mexico. They all have quite a lot in common, including their origins.

The substrate of sand reflects the geologic birth of barrier islands. Sand is ground-up quartz that is washed down large rivers. Once it enters the Gulf of Mexico, longshore currents carry it west, as a result of the Coreolis Effect. It becomes deposited parallel to the mainland shoreline and vegetates. The primary succession of millennia gone past has resulted in everything from grasslands to oak forests and the animals colonized from the mainland.

Had it not been for the discharge of several rivers flowing into Galveston Bay, we might just as well have been living on a long spit of land connecting to the mainland at High Island and the Freeport area. But the water broke through between Bolivar Peninsula and Galveston–as well as at San Luis Pass. This made an island out of our area, and a near-island of Bolivar. Even the land to the west of Galveston is called Follet's Island, and actually isn't connected to the mainland at Freeport. Plus, Rollover Pass, toward the foot of the Bolivar Peninsula, technically makes an island out of the rest of the peninsula, so one could say there are three islands.

How old is Galveston Island? To answer that, one must realize that ocean levels have been in flux for millions of years. Sixty-five million years ago, at the end of the reign of the dinosaurs, the ocean not only covered our area, it formed an inland sea all the way up through the Great Plains. Our continent's first known bird, Hesperornithes, or "western bird," was a huge, oceanic sea bird with a wing span of nearly eight feet. Its fossils came from Kansas, so it's pretty obvious that our fair home was little more than a coral reef at that time.

In the Miocene, at a time when there was a whopping 20,000 species of birds in the world, and condors with 30-foot wing spans ruled the air, a seemingly insignificant geologic episode took place. South America and North America articulated together (in the area of present-day Colombia and Panama) and remained so. This allowed many South American animals, like the lowly possum, to wander up to our neck of the woods. This pales, however, in comparison to its climatological impact.

Before the Miocene, there had been an equatorial current that flowed between our two western continents from east to west. But when the two great land masses fused, this current deflected to the north, and brought tremendous humidity to the polar regions. This moisture began the slow but inevitable process of lowering the temperature of the Northern Hemisphere. At around the beginning of the Pliocene, about 14,000,000 years ago, the earth began to cool. Finally, a little less than two million years ago, this cooling plunged our hemisphere into a series of five major ice ages and a few minor ones. A curious shake, wobble and roll to the earth, in relation to its orbit around the sun, seems to be a contributing factor in these episodes of glaciation. Some have speculated that this planetoid behavior may be linked to the apparent collision 65,000,000 years ago with some celestial body–thus ending the dinosaurs and their contemporaries. During the middle of these frigid ages, great masses of ice erupted from their oceanic spawning grounds in the far north, and rumbled slowly but destructively south through modern-day Asia, Europe and North America. Our own Appalachians were buried under a **mile** of ice! Ecosystems were entirely changed, animal distribution was totally turned upside down, and a great many species were exterminated. But possibly the greatest effect was on sea level.

When polar ice caps freeze, it takes water from the ocean and shorelines drop radically. There were places in the gulf where one could have walked out dozens of miles farther than our modern day shore! And with this drop in ocean level, the land we call Galveston Island could not have been an island. More likely, it was a high ridge on a rugged coastal plain. But it was no more an island than when this entire area was covered under sea water so long ago.

The peak of the last ice age, called the "Wisconsin" (ice ages are named for Midwestern states), was about 18,000 years ago. Since that time, as the weather has slowly warmed, ocean levels have been rising accordingly. So obviously at some point –best estimates are about 3500 years ago–gulf waters rose enough to surround this land on which we live, and make Galveston *Island*. Much of the sand that makes up Galveston Island came down the Mississippi River and west across the gulf. Also an appreciable portion came out of the Trinity River, and even the Brazos.

In spite of being isolated from the mainland for these 3500 years, the floral community still has a distinctive mainland flavor. Most of the same plants predominate, and animals as well. However, subtle changes are afoot, as geographical isolation brings on genetic isolation. One creature that I've studied, the Ground Skink, has developed differently enough from the mainland population in this time to be readily recognizable. Potentially a separate subspecies, it is only a matter of time before these secretive but common creatures become a different species. This concept is illustrative of why island populations are so important. They are potentially *all* new species in the future, but face a fragile and precarious existence on this particular island.

It would be easy to assume that there has been much deforestation on Galveston Island. While I'm a big fan of trees, and hope that much of what we have left remains here for the birds, in all honesty, most of our trees are relative newcomers. The oaks at the Laffite's Cove Nature Preserve (the old Stewart Ranch) are quite old, but most trees on the island are relatively recent additions, and the *only* original oaks are those at the Preserve.

Clearly, the island was part of an immense coastal plain grassland that held millions of Attwater Prairie Chickens and loads of other "field" species. But like so much of the mainland, prairies have been turned into cow pastures, and few species (except Becky's "Sandies") really gain from these proverbial wastelands. You cannot imagine the ecological difference between a cow pasture and a properly maintained grassland. Birds such as rare sparrows are only the beginning: There are also many species of lizards, snakes, native mice and other rodents, hundreds of arthropod species, and even some amphibians.

The wetlands we possessed on this island were as choked with water birds as any in Texas. But without the current afforded protection of the government (and I am being a bit tongue-in-cheek), much of our wetlands was filled in to create "usable" land. And this habit of manipulating land for our business is slowly turning pastures into buildings. Even worse, we are turning forests, with life-giving undergrowth, into residential areas. One by one, our native species are disappearing, and all for the almighty dollar. The island as an ecosystem is slowly

Laffite's Cove Nature Preserve

shutting down, and there will come a time we can only boast of our starlings, House Sparrows and pigeons.

The island once had wonderful grass beds on the bay side, and the diversity of creatures in these places was staggering. Now, with the high turgidity due to human activity, photosynthesis has shut down and bare bottom remains. You might think that's good for flounder, so who cares? But if we could magically produce accurate figures on what this loss has done to the seafood and fishing industry, the loss of dollars would get everyone's attention.

The island is bordered on the south side by a high-surge beach. The pounding of the waves is a selective agent that offers a home to burrowing creatures and animals who can fasten to structures in the water and hold on for dear life. Several species of game fish work the shallows, and the fishing industry benefits from the bounty. Whiting, reds, trout and drum are among the favorites caught surf fishing, which ranks way up on my list of favorite activities.

This beach is home to several species of shorebirds, found most of the year. Herring, Ring-billed and Laughing Gulls, Forster's and Royal Terns, Sanderling, Willets, Black-bellied Plovers and other assorted shorebirds rest, beachcomb or scavenge offal at the water's edge. Mole Crabs, periwinkles and larval worms hide in the sand, the latter providing an abundant food source for hungry birds.

On the bay side, away from the surge, sediments accumulate and are bound together by a series of grasses. This forms a salt marsh, one of the most valuable–and endangered– habitats on earth.

Salt marshes along Galveston Island are made up primarily of cord grass, known as *Spartina,* the genus name. Salt marshes in other parts of the gulf coast contain vast amounts of needlerush, or *Juncas.* Vast

Black-bellied Plover on the beach

acreage of Spartina once stretched along the bay side of Galveston from the east to the west end, but now is most abundant near the causeway to the mainland. More is on the way, as present areas are protected, and more marshes are now being constructed along the I-45 corridor. But we are also losing much salt marsh due to subsidence, so a battle is on.

Salt marshes are extremely productive areas. They are fed by the nutrients that wash in from rich surrounding waters, as well as any erosion from uphill. Water, obviously essential for primary productivity, is in large supply, as is sunlight. Although the productivity of salt marshes is tempered by the plant's need to pump salt out of their roots, you will find salt marshes a fascinating place, teeming with life and all its rich smells.

The vast majority of game fish rely on salt marshes for their reproduction. The destruction of salt marshes, conversely, spells doom for commercial and sport fishing interests. These marshes now have statutory protection, although Texas does not exactly "lead the way" in wetland protection and enforcement. But the dangerous dredge and fill practices that ran wild in past years seem to be curtailed, and slowly we are moving in a right direction to protect critical ecosystems.

In addition to game fish reproducing, there are several species of "minnows" that live out their lives in salt marshes. The tidal creeks bring their life-giving yummies from the open water, and fish such as mollies, killifish and sheepshead minnow (all collectively called "mud minnow," etc.) feast on the buffet. These in turn, invite huge numbers of water birds, salt marsh snakes, raccoon and other picivores into the marsh. It is not uncommon to see flocks of several hundred egrets, herons and ibis scooping up a fishy lunch at any time of the year.

A flourishing salt marsh near East Beach

Joining the fish are invertebrates like crabs all through the salt marsh, especially in tidal creeks. These feed on detritus (dead and rotting animal and plant matter) and also offer a delicacy for some of the predators lurking along the shore. Periwinkle Snails climb the cord grass, scraping bacteria off the stem, staying out of the Blue Crab's way at high tide. And fiddler crabs scurry along the mudflats scraping up bacteria-laden sand, and, after sifting out these microbes, leave tiny balls of discarded sand as reminders of their presence.

Possibly the most notable invertebrate in this habitat is the Salt Marsh Mosquito. Many areas go months with little activity from these vampires, but after heavy rains, when their eggs hatch, veritable clouds of bloodsuckers fan out from the marshes to seek a meal of hemoglobin. We must remind ourselves that they, in turn, form an important food source for many insectivorous creatures, and their larvae do the same for aquatic hunters, such as small fish. But I don't think we are in any danger of exterminating these "Hemo Goblins."

Several mammals are frequently found in salt marshes, such as raccoons, because shellfish are a readily available food source. Some birds are *only* found in salt marshes, and their continued presence on this planet depend on us maintaining healthy homes for them. A chicken-like bird called the Clapper Rail is quite abundant in our marshes, though it is heard far more than seen. A loud "ick ick ick ick..." reverberates over the cord grass, and tells of this fiddler crab-eating, camouflaged creature that slips unobtrusively through marsh grass with the stealth of a ghost. They and the Seaside Sparrow will truly become ghosts if our salt marshes fail to exist, or if they lose their quality and diversity.

Tidal Creek

The soil type of the island is, of course, very sandy. This, and the presence of so much salt in the substrate, creates desert-like conditions. Water percolates quickly between the large grains of sand, so standing water may at times be hard to find. This dry aspect leads to many of the plants and animals associated with deserts, such as rattlesnakes, cactus, nettles, black widows, scrubby plants, racerunners, caracaras and Spanish Bayonet.

This is poor soil for farming, so much of the land is used for pasturing cattle. Some creatures like Sandhill Cranes and "grasspipers" utilize this habitat, but by and large, it's pretty worthless to wildlife. But it *is* preferable to miles and miles of condos and asphalt, so the west end of the island stays fairly wild and not unscenic.

Relatively wild areas may be found at the Laffite's Cove Nature Preserve, and a few isolated spots between town and the west end. Also, Pelican Island, the Apfell Park area, and land just west of East beach offer desolate grasslands for those seeking nature. But by and large, the natural heritage of Galveston Island has gone the way of the bulldozer. And that is precisely the reason we must do everything in our power to save what remains for future generations.

Boardwalk over marsh leading to the Preserve

CHAPTER **3:** **Marine**
Invertebrates in Galveston Waters

The animals with whom we are most familiar have two characteristics. One is they're usually land animals, and the other is they usually have a backbone. Therefore, creatures like birds, mammals and reptiles get an awful lot of our attention.

But out in the murky depths surrounding our fair island exist an incredible assortment of strange marine animals that few islanders comprehend. Some lie buried in the mud, some cling to fixed or floating objects, while others drift freely with the tides. And though there are many differences in this varied community, these marine creatures all have one thing in common: they have no backbone.

Now, please forgive a little classification lesson. All animals are divided into 27 groups we call phyla. All vertebrates we know–fish, amphibians, reptiles, birds and mammals–are all in one of these phyla (Chordata) with a few invertebrates like sea squirts. So really, the vast majority of all animals are invertebrates, and the vast majority of the invertebrate phyla are marine. On land, besides the vertebrates, there are some Arthropods (like insects and spiders), some worms (like our earthworms and hard-to-find flatworms) and a few mollusks (like snails and slugs). But that is nothing compared to the vast assemblage of marine invertebrates.

This means about two dozen or more of the 27 phyla are marine, and that means that by far the greatest *disparity* of animals is in the ocean. Disparity refers to differences in body structure–the very stuff on which classification is built. On land, there is a great diversity of insects, actually about half the species of animals in the world. But they are all pretty similar: three body parts, six legs, wings, and so forth. But with oceanic phyla, there are radically different creatures living side by side–often attached to each other–representing more disparity than on all the land masses on earth! In this chapter, these phyla (except worms) will be large, underlined boldface. The classes that make up the phyla will be simply boldfaced, to make classification easier.

Recently I found a pen shell (phylum Mollusca) with a tube worm on it (phylum Annelida). There was a tiny cloak anemone (phylum Coelenterata) right beside the worm track and barnacles all over the shell (phylum Arthropoda). Wow, that's four phyla of creatures–each with bodies that were radically different–all living together. I don't believe I have ever seen more than four phyla of animals on land in my life!

Of course, sea creatures had a head start. The Cambrian Explosion, where invertebrates got their start, was over 600,000,000 years ago. So they have been around roughly twice as long as land animals. And for whatever reason, there have been no new phyla of animals since the first land animals came about, in the late Paleozoic. The amazing thing is that many of our coolest sea creatures were land animals that returned to the sea, becoming radically different in their form. These are whales, dolphins, sea snakes, sea turtles, marine iguanas, manatee, many birds, and a few other beasts. A lot of folks in Galveston have pretty much returned to the sea, as well!

It is hard to imagine how different ocean life is from a terrestrial existence. First, sound waves travel infinitely farther in water than on land. Our whales, for instance, can hear each another hundreds of miles away! Another weird thing is living in a 3D world. On land, we basically think about what's in front of us, or maybe to the sides. We spend very little thought on what's under us, or in the air over us. But in the ocean, danger and food can come from any direction, and natural selection weeded out marine animals that don't look down a long time ago. Fish lurking in the mud or sandy bottom were agents of this selection (predators so frequently serve in this role).

The ocean is a far less stressful environment for animals to live in than land. For instance, there is only a gradual change in temperature with the seasons. On land, our temperature can drop twenty or thirty degrees in a 24-hour period. In the ocean, salinity and moisture stay the same, whereas one downpour can turn a dry rat into a drowned rat in a hurry. And think of the poor frog that carelessly jumps into salt water. The change in salt could turn it into "amphibiprune."

All in all, the ocean is a peaceful, gentle place to live, compared to land. And it's full of a bounty of extraordinary life that hides secrets that will astound you. But to write on all the life in the sea around Galveston would take volumes. We will take six major phyla, and outline their members that can be found with regularity along our lagoons, canals, bays and open gulf. The fantastic life histories of these primitive animals will amaze and interest you.

Sponges are by far our most primitive animals. In fact, they weren't even considered animals until about a century ago. The confusion was compounded by the fact many sponges have algae growing within them, so these greenish, plant-looking things weren't very animal-like. But they respire with oxygen, release carbon dioxide, and have cell membranes. They're animals.

Sponges are in essence a colony of undifferentiated cells, acting as a net. Together, these cells filter the water and catch microscopic bits of food. They absorb them extracellularly, and most likely have a metabolism like that of Jabba the Hutt. They grow on fixed objects in the sea, and will "reproduce" by budding. This is when they "deliberately" break off a tiny portion of themselves, and it grows into a new sponge wherever it lands and attaches.

Sponges came from one-celled organisms like amoebas hundreds of millions of years ago. These tiny microbes began attaching to each other, and this strategy worked as they could catch more food cooperatively than individually. For quite some time, nature experimented with larger and larger colonies of these one-celled fellows, until certain set sizes seemed to work best.

When sponges came about, they had to make their bodies out of something in the natural environment. Some used calcium and others used silicon. This is why some of our sponges even today are comprised of calcium carbonate (like a lot of sea creatures) and others are made of silicon dioxide. Their chemical makeup partly determines which class of sponges each one is.

Around Galveston, most of our sponges are the calcium carbonate variety, like basket sponges. It is not easy to simply go out and find them, as they live often on the bottom of a murky water column. But with all the organic materials in our waters, life as a Galveston sponge is a veritable smorgasbord. Occasionally, one of these creatures washes up on the beach, and we can see what lies in the depths of our bays and gulf.

Sponges often represent whole communities of animals. It is easy to bore through many sponges, so within its body may lie worms, small fish, tiny crabs, snapping shrimp, and many other animals that we say are living *commensally* with the sponge. This makes sponges a keystone species because of their importance to other groups of animals, and thus makes their continued existence necessary.

Coelenterates. This is a strange name for a common group of sea creatures. The name of the phylum above means "hollow gut," which pretty well describes their primitive form. They are also called **Cnidaria** by some authorities, which means "nettle." They are a mass of jelly-like tissue with a large cavity in the middle for digestion. Surrounding their mouth are tentacles that serve to stun and gather food (or sting the living heck out of bathers). So now you realize we are talking about jellyfish, and also anemones. They have no brain, or other systems, but have a net of nerves surrounding them that senses their environment. They are divided into two separate ecological groups, one living at the top and the other on the bottom of the sea.

Jellyfish comprise a class of animals within Coelenterata called Syphozoa, which means "cup animal." Indeed, they are shaped like an upside-down cup (with those nasty tentacles around the opening), floating along with the currents. Galveston residents are acutely aware of the "cabbage head" or "cannon ball" variety that sometimes beach themselves in huge numbers. And other than providing a food source for a few shorebirds, they are quite a public nuisance.

Anemones are actually much like jellyfish, except they are attached to the bottom with the tentacles up in the water column, rather than floating on the surface with tentacles hanging down. But anemones are harmless, because the barbs in their stinging cells are so short, they can't penetrate human skin. Obviously, many jellyfish can, making them "an enemy." :)

Cannonball and Sargasso Weed

Our common anemone is the **Cloak Anemone**. It is easily found on any debris washed in along the shoreline, and looks like a grey cone. Many times you can see orange threads coming out the top, and the anemone might be in various stages of being closed up. They can also be found on rock jetties in crevices, often exposed to air at low tides. Good luck getting them out, though, as their "holdfast" (basal disk) is like superglue. They do well in aquaria, though, when found on objects that make their removal possible. Their class name is Anthozoa, which means "flower animal." Indeed, many species look like flowers growing under the sea. Scientists refer to any Coelenterate that lives such a life (including Coral) as a polyp. Those that float freely like jellyfish are referred to as medusa, after the unfortunate lady in mythology with snakes for hair.

One of the most unique creatures in the animal kingdom is the Man of War. These fierce tropical medusa float in after long periods of southerly wind, and terrorize all who enter the water. The exceptionally long tentacles may wrap around swimmers, and inflict brutal pain. About twice a year, tremendous numbers of Man of War wash up on Galveston beaches and litter the sand with thousands of bluish balloons. These are the organs that hold air and keep the animal floating. It often holds air for days on end, making great fun for passersby who pop them unceremoniously with their feet. A very short time after beaching, both these and jellyfish are rendered harmless.

Man of War are probably the most unique organism in the world. They are actually made up of several different animals, all living and working as one creature. Each part reproduces its own part; for example, the bell makes other bells. There is nothing like it on earth! So the next time you curse these inconvenient, sometimes painful creatures, just remember what an incredible form of life they actually are. But don't go out and hug one, either.

Worms do not constitute one phylum, but rather several. The most abundant group of worms is **Polychaeta**, a class of segmented worms (Annelida) that occurs many places in the ocean in staggering numbers. As adults, they burrow into the sand, leaving small, cone-shaped domes that may be seen all over low tide flats. The adults are predators that hide in the burrow and rise to the surface instantly to grab unsuspecting invertebrate prey and drag them down for lunch.

The larvae of Polychaetes are as numerous as any animal in our seas, and provide an important food source for zillions of predators. They are a few inches long, and when viewed up close, the telltale "many spines" (the meaning of *polychaete*) may be seen sticking out the sides, not unlike the body of the ill-tempered centipede of our woodlands. They are quite harmless as larvae, and are terribly interesting for kids when viewed under any kind of dissecting scope—or binoculars held backwards (a cute birdwatcher's trick).

Polychaetes are in the phylum Annelida (Segmented Worms), which includes earthworms and leeches (leeches are generally freshwater creatures, and may not occur on Galveston). They all have segments, and also a curious circle about their body, which gives the phylum the name Annelida, or "little ring." The maximum size for both earthworms and polychaetes is around a yard (!), and gives us pause to be thankful that leeches don't get that big.

Segmented worms are monoecious, meaning each individual has both sets of sex organs. These hermaphrodites mate on the third of the complete-looking moons each month, around an hour after dark. They clasp and practice reciprocal fertilization, rolling around in the surf all night and glowing red. This peculiar form of bioluminescence has earned them the name "fire worm."

Flatworms, phylum Platyhelminthes, are poorly represented in Galveston waters. They are flat, mobile, and often brightly colored creatures that freely swim the world's tropical oceans. They also occur as endoparasites, much to the dismay of many pets. But they are on the direct line of evolution to much higher phyla of animals as well, including ours, the Chordates.

There are other phyla of worms in the sea, such as Ribbon Worms and Roundworms, which will not be explored in this work. As a "super phylum," worms are hailed as the first creatures to really move in a direction under their own power. Over the eons, evolution sculpted their shape to become elongate, rather than having the radial symmetry of Coelenterates, or the odd irregular symmetry of the sponges.

Radial symmetry is useful for feeding when an animal is getting lunch by contacting the environment. But purposefully moving calls for a more streamlined shape, thus creating bilateral form. In bilateral symmetry, like virtually all vertebrates, there is an anterior (front end), also a posterior (rear end), and two approximately equal sides. The all-important sensing organs are in the anterior of the creature, so they will know what's ahead before sticking their head into the waiting claws of a Stone Crab. Animals with bilateral symmetry also have a dorsum (top), venter (bottom), and some, like us, walk on two legs, which confuses everything.

Echinoderms also possess radial symmetry, at least as adults, as they also feed by contacting their environment. They are woefully slow, and unfortunately not as common around Galveston as in many parts of the Gulf of Mexico. Although the name might be somewhat unfamiliar to the neophyte, many of their classes, like starfish, will ring bells for sure.

The name "echinoderm" denotes spiny skin, which about covers it. Some, like sea urchins have a coating of huge spines, while others' spines are more diminutive. In addition, echinoderms have a curious arrangement of five body parts: five arms on brittle stars and starfish, radial canals numbering five (along with many other body parts), and even patterns of five similar designs on the flat bodies of sand dollars. We can put a man on the moon, but scientists don't have a clue why such an unlikely and rare number in the animal kingdom as five turns up so frequently in one phylum of animals.

Echinoderms also have a water vascular system that changes water pressure all over their bodies, thus making arms and other parts move. It is not unlike the hydraulics of spiders. This system is useful in allowing a special adaptation to function: the tubed feet. These straw-like projections cling to objects (sometimes food) by forming a suction on the end by decreasing pressure in the tubes. It is similar to sucking on a straw and placing the end on our hand.

But echinoderms may be most famous for their powers of regeneration. If an arm of a starfish is broken off, it simply grows back. If a sea cucumber is broken open, it closes and heals as if the injury never happened. We can make nuclear bombs, but cannot figure out how to get our own bodies to regenerate–even though each cell has the genetic information for the entire body.

The flagship of the echinoderms would be **starfish**. These voracious predators are not common in the area, but are occasionally seen washed up on the beach. They are supposed to have five arms, though some have fewer, which could be disarming. However, they even have the ability to use a particular arm when desired, supposedly because sometimes a certain arm is missing, and they need to be able to control which arm is in use.

Starfish eat many things, but their favorite food is bivalves like clams, oysters and scallops. They grab the mollusk with the tubed feet of their arms, and exert constant pressure to open the two shells. This is no contest at first, but eventually the muscle of the bivalve begins to tire, and there will develop a small opening between the two shells. At this point, the stomach of the starfish *everts* (leaves its body on a gut) and enters the bivalve through the opening. The stomach digests the soft body of the bivalve, leaving only two shells on the ocean bottom as evidence of the struggle.

Brittlestars are not closely related to starfish, as they have spindly arms like a snake's tail (named for this likeness as *Ophiuroidea*, "snake tail"), and a pentagonal basal disk where their organs are located. These small creatures can be incredibly abundant, but local. They are limber, and can, in fact, swim with their arms. They eat rotten material on the sea floor.

Sometimes a fish or other predator attacks a brittlestar that is swimming. The brittlestar will pop off its basal disk and its guts ease out into the water. As the fish gobbles up the tender morsels, the arms and shell of the victim drop to the bottom, only to regenerate the guts and move on. In a scant couple of weeks, it will again have the guts for that clever trick.

Sea urchins are the pin cushions of the ocean. Their long, sharp spines make them impervious to most attacks, as they slowly move through grasses and along the sea floor. Urchin numbers have been greatly reduced by the loss of sea grass habitat, along with many other species that utilize grasses for food, shelter, or the physical structure.

In the orient, urchins are used for food, as the gonads are considered a delicacy. They are also very important in science/medical research, as their eggs are extremely large and easy to study in development. They do form an important food source for a few fish, who have learned how to flip them over and attack the soft underside. Once they have been killed and wash in to shore, the "Aristotle's lantern" (a five-sided, cone-shaped structure) may be found within the shell.

Sea Cucumbers are grotesque creatures, six inches long and shaped about like a large dill pickle. They have rows of tubed feet running down their bodies, and openings at both ends. They live in the sand or mud of the bottom, and feed on organic material along the bottom (deposit feeder). Entering through the openings of both ends are tiny creatures like diminutive crabs and other midgets, using the cucumber for an organic place to live.

When sea cucumbers are attacked, they have one of the most bizarre defenses known to man. At first contact, they will writhe their bodies around like they are sick, which discourages some who would attack. If that doesn't work, cracks appear all over their torso, allowing an array of nasty body juices to emerge into the water. If this fails to run off the predator, their bodies break open further, and various organs and guts are discharged. This is often done in concert with the spitting out of white, viscous tubes that stick to the aggressor like liquid string shot out of a can.

Up to this point, our hero can recover, regenerating its losses as the weeks roll past. But if all the above fails to dissuade the intruder, they will essentially disintegrate into a pitiful blob of protoplasm, effectively committing suicide. There are virtually no animals who will touch this disgusting mass, and the dead cucumber has successfully continued the tradition of no predator *relying* on their kind as a food source. I must say, having witnessed this stomach-turning act, that one very hungry Blue Crab, surely having the least amount of pride of all the scavengers, did in fact take a small quantity of these briny remains (in a classroom touch tank), for several agonizing minutes. But he clearly did not like it. :(

Mollusks are an incredibly abundant phylum of largely sea creatures, with only a few snails and slugs venturing into freshwater and terrestrial habitats. Their name comes from the Greek word for soft (mollis), though most have extremely hard shells covering the delectable animal itself. Anything that tastes as good as an oyster, clam or scallop *better* have a hard shell!

The above delicacies are **bivalves**, far and away the largest population of this phylum. There are also gastropods (normally shaped like snails), cephalopods (like octopus and squid), and some that are not widely known to the average beachcomber. Mollusk shells decorate our beaches, and are an important food source for a plethora of creatures.

Bivalves are tasty morsels with two identical shells. They attach to hard structures, make large colonies like oyster reefs, or lie buried in the mud like cockles. Being tasty and abundant, they have set themselves up as an important food source, and even some land animals like raccoons and oystercatchers (and the author) find them irresistible. To compensate for heavy losses, most females lay thousands–and even millions–of eggs in a season. Although few make it to adulthood, this sure qualified them for a laboratory in natural selection!

Oysters are the keystone species in a very important community within the marine realm. Oyster reefs are found in many areas where low surge occurs, so they are more often found on the bay side of the island. Hundreds of thousands of oysters live stuck together in elongate reefs and their presence invites many other species of animals to cohabitate. Most of the phyla and even classes discussed in this work are found in oyster reefs, and reefs ensure a continued diversity for the waters of Galveston. It is great fun to pick through a clump of oysters to see what's there, but be careful–they are very sharp. Hands and feet may suffer if you are careless.

Gastropods are voracious hunters, whose class name means "stomach-foot." They have a large muscular foot protruding from their shell, with a scraping radula built in for removing scraps of meat from shells and carcasses. Sometimes called univalves, they have one shell, normally in some fashion like a familiar snail. Many call them marine snails.

When a gastropod attacks a bivalve, it doesn't rely on stamina and cleverness like the starfish. It simply rips open the shell with its muscular foot, and scrapes out the meat with its radula. Then the creature buries itself and lies dormant for weeks in the substrate. When it is hungry, it will emerge and find another victim (sometimes another gastropod) and go back to sleep.

Our state shell is the Lightning Whelk, which is common and widespread. But it is different in one key way from all our other gastropods. When held with the large end up, its opening is on the left side. All others are "right-handed." The story of how they got that way is both interesting and an excellent example of artificial selection.

According to fossils, and Native American trash piles called "middens," early "Indians" used to eat Lightning Whelks like crazy. And the vast majority of these whelks were right-handed, like other gastropod species we have today. But a few were apparently mutations, and were left-handed. It was considered bad luck to eat these evil, *sinistral* whelks, so the left-handed ones weren't harvested.Over the past few thousand years, the Native Americans, who gathered much of their food from our shores, pretty well eliminated the right-handed ones. So today, these whelks are left-handed because of man, and are a textbook example of artificial selection.

There are quite a few other species of gastropods around Galveston waters, and their shells are easily found on the beach. Terrestrial slugs are rare on the island because of its salty flavor, and snails are normally of an introduced variety, and despised by gardeners. However, in the salt marshes, periwinkles are abundant, scraping bacteria off cordgrass stems with their radula as they ease along. They, in turn, offer a morsel for the always hungry Blue Crab.

Cephalopods are probably more common around the island than many people would suspect. Around East Beach, squid are seined up frequently for scientific research. Octopus lurk around docks and in oyster beds, watching for their favorite food, the crabs. Both have the ability to jet along through the gulf squirting water out their siphon, although octopus prefer creeping along on the bottom on their abundance of "legs."

These two creatures are remarkably advanced invertebrates. They have excellent eyes, with the octopus, especially, having a surprisingly well developed brain. Their tentacles are armed with suction cups for grabbing their prey, and both have the ability to change color (although octopus can actually change the *texture* of its skin to match the surrounding material!). Cephalopoda means head-foot, which certainly describes these muscular animals. However, there are some key differences in the two, mainly due to their habitat and niche.

Living on the bottom and taking on Blue Crabs make octopus strong, but slow. Their ability to match their surroundings is renowned, and more amazing is the way they can slip through slight cracks in rocks, boards, and tops of aquaria! They have eight tentacles (compared to the squid's ten) and their beak is heavy enough to crunch right through a large crab shell. When handled, octopus are benign, but their suckers feel pretty strange to the uninitiated. One word of caution: the tiny dwarf octopus will bite the cold living daylights out anyone who picks them up!

Squid are free swimmers, and chase fish for meals. They are, therefore, quite streamlined, and much faster than their cousin the octopus. They often school in large numbers, also unlike the solitary octopus. And though their beak is very effective on fish, they are quite inoffensive when handled. They will almost surely die if you capture them and place them in a tank.

A class represented by one abundant mollusk is the **Chiton**. These creatures are found clinging to shells and wood in our waters, and are segmented, like the rollie pollies in our yards. When pried off, you can see the muscular foot below, and see the meat that, in the much larger Caribbean species, is eaten and called "sea beef." Chitons are seldom over an inch long in our waters.

The **Arthropods** comprise well over half the species in the world. The major class is the insects, which are poorly represented in the water, especially salt water. But one class of these "jointed-legged" animals is quite common in the sea, and that is the **Crustaceans**. This class is comprised of shrimp, lobster, crayfish (freshwater), barnacles, and a host of crabs. Crustaceans have hard exoskeletons made of chitin (crusta=hard), which, considering how they taste, is a good thing. They also have a number of pairs of appendages, used for a variety of purposes.

In terms of crabs, Galveston has the usual suspects to be found on the gulf coast. The economically important Blue Crabs live off-shore until the breeding season when they come to our shoreline in droves in summer to spawn. Crabbing is then done commercially, as well as for recreation. Note, though, that the "sponge" crabs (those females carrying the orange eggs) are illegal to harvest. This ensures a bounty of crabs the next year and keeps crabbers from getting in a "pinch."

Blue Crabs are as hearty as they are ill-tempered. They frequently survive attacks by large predators, either by courage or trickery. They put up a great fight, but when all seems lost, they pop off a pincher for a treat. While the enemy is devouring the claw, the crab gets away. This process is called *autotomy*, where a part of the body is sacrificed for the creature's life. Their last enemy is the cold, which they escape by moving to deep water in fall.

Fiddler crabs are interesting little creatures. The males are distinguished by their long claw (the fiddle), and the females have two small ones. The males use the claw for signaling females, but it does not make much of a defense. If you watch their behavior, you might witness the male convincing the female to descend into one of their burrows, where they make the next generation.

Fiddler crabs are widely used as fish bait, such as for sheepshead. This pressure, along with habitat loss, has greatly reduced the population of this animal in our area. Fishermen are urged to take only a reasonable amount of crabs for bait,

iddler Crabs near their burrows

and to turn loose those that are unused. Fiddler crabs may live for a day or so away from their haunt, but will perish if kept too long.

Hermit crabs are abundant in Galveston waters, and are benign, interesting creatures for kids to investigate. They take over an empty shell of a dead gastropod, and their abdomen fits snugly in the circular opening within the shell. They walk around on their appendages, looking for morsels on which to feed. Rather than pinching, like their ill-tempered cousins, they simply retreat into their shell, until they lose their fear–usually after a short time.

In our area, three species of hermit crabs predominate. The tiny Dwarf Hermit is found in droves all along our shallow waters, and is scarcely bigger than a marble. The Flat-clawed Hermit is larger, and covers its opening with the flat claw when it retreats. Last is the robust Stripe-clawed Hermit, which drags along looking for dead bits of animal flesh, and is easily identified by its large size and stripes.

A very ancient creature, the horseshoe crab, has been roaming the bottom of the world's oceans for about four hundred million years, relatively unchanged. Like their trilobite ancestor, their niche is to look for bits of rotten flesh or vegetation on the sea floor for a scant diet. But sometimes they come ashore to breed, where they deposit thousands of eggs in the sand. The female has a smaller male in tow, who fertilizes the eggs.

These harmless animals are quite unique, as they are somewhat unrelated to other arthropods. The stiff tail, called a *telson,* is used to point *toward* an intruder, thus keeping it at bay. But this same tail makes a great handle, and children can play with these crabs unmolested. Their curious eyes are compound, and their bizarre appendages fill kids' eyes full of wonder.

Shrimp are also crustaceans, like crabs, but are built very differently. They are elongate, with a zillion pairs of legs and two very long antennae. Shrimp swim forward slowly using their legs, but can swim backwards in quick bursts with their tail.

Their "shell," a plastic-like carapace, is some protection, but shrimp are eaten by about half the creatures in the sea! Like many species of marine organisms, they survive by reproducing like crazy.

Speaking of reproducing, Brown Shrimp and Pink Shrimp (in smaller numbers) lay eggs around twenty miles out in late spring. Larvae swim around to the bay side and grow up there for a couple of months. Then, they head out the passes for deep water where they will mature and return after a year to spawn themselves. They seldom ever see their second year of life.

White Shrimp spawn later, almost in midsummer, and much closer to shore. This is a good time for them to be around, because the bay is closed to shrimping at that time. They mature in fall and head out to open water like the Brown and Pink Shrimp. The largest shrimp get close to nine inches (yummy), but this is rare. In fact, probably a very small minority ever sees adulthood, and the chance to contribute to a new generation.

Barnacles seem like a pretty insignificant crustacean, unless you've stepped on them barefoot, or had them grow all over your property. But they are really interesting creatures, and fascinating to observe. They grow in colonies on many surfaces, although they seem to prefer wood.

Barnacles are essentially an upside-down shrimp, buried within a cup-shaped, very hard casing they emit. They lay on their back filtering the water with their *cirri*, which are modified appendages with feather-like edges. When danger comes, they close two small "doors" that cover the opening of the cup, and are usually safe and secure from danger. However, there are enemies that can penetrate the doors, and this spells doom for the helpless creature.

How these stationary animals mate is interesting. Most immobile creatures of the sea simply release their gametes (eggs and sperm) into the water at an agreed upon time and fertilization takes place by chance in the briny swarm. But male barnacles have a long appendage for mating that takes its spermataphore (packet of sperm) and suddenly thrusts it in place on the neighboring gal, and fertilization is direct and quick. She probably never knew what hit her. Fertilized eggs are then released and the larvae attach and grow into new barnacles.

The phylum **Chordata** is normally thought of as creatures with backbones, and certainly the vast majority are vertebrates. But within the murky depths of our waters lie strange life forms that fit the Chordate criteria (at least part of a spinal cord *sometime* during their lifetime) and have some fairly interesting life history.

Sea squirts are plump little creatures that live on rocks, wooden structures and other substrates they can cling to. They look like tan raisins, short and puffy. Sea squirts are filter feeders, sucking in water, taking out microbes and nutrients, and squirting the filtered water out. They have fat bodies and small mouths at the top, and do not move.

Sea squirts are in the subphylum *Urochordata*, meaning they have their spinal cord in their tail. But of course, adults have no tail! Their tadpole-like larvae have a portion of a spinal cord for movement, and once a larvae is attached and begins to grow into an adult squirt, the tail is absorbed as food. Amazingly, the mouth begins as the attachment to the dock (or whatever), and as squirts transform, their mouth begins moving day by day 180 degrees to where the tail was! Now the mouth sticks out into the water column, just like the tail once did, and filter feeds.

These are also called tunicates, for the "tunic" (robe) monks wear. This covering is made from the cellulose they metabolize from microscopic plants digested. It is a very thick, tough coating that protects them from a variety of would-be predators. Blue Crabs have been known to pick at them, but they must be pretty hungry! Some people get a kick out of breaking off sea squirts and squeezing them, thus squirting water on their friends. This probably kills the creatures, though, and should be discouraged.

We have other invertebrate chordates that are rarely seen, like lancelets, but are encountered so seldom that they do not bear discussion. However, it should be evident that Galveston waters teem with variety and disparity of invertebrate marine life.

One fun activity is to seine a tidal creek or other portion of salt water to see the abundance of small fish (and invertebrates) that live in our waters. Some of the minnows may be used as bait for game fish; or little portable aquaria may be set up in the shade for children to study marine life for a few minutes, before release. A handful of these, along with a couple of hermit crabs make a nice permanent aquarium in the home.

One tiny ecological community that is terribly interesting and that kids LOVE is the Sargasso Weed that drifts in during the warm season. This "seaweed" (Red Algae) comes our way from the middle of the Atlantic Ocean, floating along on currents, blown by wind. It certainly is not a big favorite of the beach/tourism industry, as Galveston spends thousands of dollars annually to scrape it off the beach to make things more attractive for our visitors. Although I find no great fault in this practice, I will say that it's likely an awful lot of sand is removed every time we "scrape," and this almost certainly leads to the loss of beach sand.

But the great thing about the thousands of little clumps of Sargasso Weed is that they bring tiny creatures with them, floating along in the small masses of vegetation. Shrimp, crabs, sea slugs and various fishes all live within the algae, feeding, hiding and even reproducing, on their way to the New World! And what is even more amazing is that they are colored *exactly* like the algae itself! This is a textbook example of (at least) cryptic coloration, if not mimicry.

You parents out there: If you ever get a chance, take your child down to the shoreline when the Sargasso is floating in and scoop it up with a fine-meshed pool net and carefully remove the weed. The tiny animals that are left behind make for a neat glimpse at nature's secret magic at work, and will delight and stimulate the mind of your excited child. Truth be told, I've known a few adults who couldn't get enough of this... :)

It should also be mentioned that the piles of this "seaweed" serve as a tremendous food source for migratory shorebirds such as Ruddy Turnstones, Dunlins, Sanderlings and others. My notion is that the aforementioned passengers fall off at the shoreline, and the resulting beach hoppers (amphipods) and other invertebrates that congregate at the piles of seaweed are the attraction.

For more detailed information about these marine invertebrates and their habitats, try *Shore Ecology of the Gulf of Mexico* by Britton and Morton.

CHAPTER 4: **Galveston:
Fisherman's Paradise**

Fish are the main reason shrimp seldom reach maturity. And there is a bounty of fish, both in terms of species as well as numbers, in Galveston waters. Game fish may be caught at any time of the year, although the late winter months are less productive.

Sportfishing is a two billion dollar industry on the Texas coast annually, and Galveston is one of the most popular sites, due in part to its close proximity to Houston. In addition, the value of commercial fishing in the bay and gulf around Galveston annually is over 30 million dollars. Therefore, the value of the fishing industry cannot be overstated.

The **Red Drum**, or "redfish" is one of the most popular game fish on the entire gulf coast. Large females, ironically called "bull reds," may approach a yard in length! They may be caught from the rough seas of the gulf side to the calm inlets and canals on the north side of the island. In the cold of winter, they may be caught in the deep waters of the bay side. They put up a great fight, and are delicious. Reds are a golden color with a few conspicuous dark spots near the tail.

These great gamefish take a variety of bait. Many use cut bait on large rods, especially in the San Luis Pass area. They will also take lures such as spoons along canal edges and over grass, though some of the big ones may be wary of artificials. Many people, though, catch reds on live shrimp, a couple of feet below a cork. Occasionally, reds are caught on dead shrimp on the bottom, much like what people use for whiting. But sometimes overlooked is their love for small crabs, caught in the shallows. Using any bait, though, redfish are never timid about grabbing the hook and letting you know there's something on the line!

Whiting are also not shy about grabbing a line. Most of these tasty fish are caught in the surf on dead shrimp, fished on the bottom. You may use a fairly heavy weight for the pounding surf, as they will pull hard enough to feel it. Fresh shrimp works better than older bait, and I suggest you peel the shrimp and thread it on a medium-sized hook. Peeling it keeps the fish from tearing off the peel and knocking the shrimp off the hook.

Whiting, named for their cryptic coloration on the sandy bottom, are something one can catch in winter. Some individuals get fairly large by late winter, but then leave the small ones to man the surf in spring. Their light meat is excellent when fresh, although they normally do not attain a large size. But the fight is a strong one, and they are faithfully found most of the year.

Speckled Trout are a warm water phenomenon. My favorite way to catch them is to wade out into the surf or bay side and use live shrimp and a cork. Try to fish where the water is fairly clear and a rising or high tide may work best. But ask around in the various bait shops because trout move around and sometimes one area may be hot hot hot for a few days. For fishing the West End, I always ask directions from Jerry and Becky at West Bay Bait and Tackle, about a mile west of Jamaica Beach (409) 737-2908.

Trout fishing is a real art which many people have perfected. They will sometimes shun using live bait and go with soft plastics or top water lures. These folks work the canals and grassbeds on the north side (Bay) of the island, and often get their limit in an hour or two of fishing.

Black Drum are closely related to redfish (Red Drum) and may attain a large size as well. These guys hit our beach fronts in early spring and spawn in the near beach. They are shaped as a tall fish, with broad, dark bars running down their sides. They love peeled shrimp, and put up a good fight. They become scarce during the warm months, but reappear in late fall with a vengeance. Black Drum may be caught on the bay side as well, and will take crabs, like their red cousins.
Golden Croaker don't get the notoriety of some of the larger

game fish, but their light, delicate meat is delicious, and they may be caught in big numbers in early spring. During this time, you may see docks lined with those seeking croaker, and the bounty is great. They take dead shrimp on the bottom, and fight hard for their diminutive size.

Flounder are as odd as they are delicious. Their light, flakey meat is "flat" good, but their looks make them a strange sight for the uninitiated. They are *depressed*, like a sting ray, and hide very well on the bottom. But from this camouflaged fish comes terrible jaws with huge teeth and a ravenous appetite. They take lures, dead shrimp, and especially live "minnows" in a heartbeat, and provide a good fight with their flat, muscular bodies.

Flounder-like fish (tonguefish, sole, halibut) are unique in the vertebrate world. They are the only creatures with backbones that do not have bilateral symmetry (where both sides of the body are equal). Since through their evolution they were essentially turned "sideways," their brain is on one side and their mouth is on the other. Not even sting rays are like this.

All spring, flounder begin filling up the bay side of the island, and may be gigged in the warm months at night with a strong light. Bring lots of mosquito repellant, as you may not be the only creature out there looking for a meal.

Flounder may be caught virtually any time of the year, but are highly sought during the flounder run in late fall, where they seem to migrate from the bay to the gulf through the passes. At this time, dozens of fishermen may be seen lined up along San Luis Pass, dangling their bait into the current. **This is a very dangerous place to fish**, and those who cannot swim should *not even think* about wading in these strong, unpredictable currents. The west side of the pass is an even worse place to wadefish, and is not as good for flounder, either. Flounder are best caught at this time after strong "northers," which begin running them out of the bay.

Sheepshead are locally common around pilings, rocks, and other structures. They have molar-like teeth, and gnaw at barnacles and other mollusks. Because of this and their small mouths, they're not easy to catch. One should use a small hook and an even smaller piece of shrimp. One proven method of catching sheepshead is to slowly work a dock, dropping dead shrimp along the underwater structure. This may also catch flounder, but the down side is that many small fish like the pesky pinfish go after the shrimp. A solution (as well as some retribution) is to catch the pinfish and put them out on a larger rod with a cork, inviting a large game fish to have lunch.

Mullet are an extremely important fish in our area. Many large fish (and dolphins) feed on this species, and the numbers support this predation. We also catch them and use them for bait in the huge sport fishing industry. Large ones are cut up, but small live mullet are about as tempting as any bait out there. And watch out–some pretty healthy hombres will grab baby mullet on your line, and you better buckle up!

East of the Mississippi, fresh mullet are considered delicious and are eaten by the tons. But the sediments of this great river are carried westward, toward us, by longshore currents, and make these deposit feeders grainy. So they remain fish food in Galveston.

Various species of **gar** are caught in Galveston waters, although few people (except my crazy brother) actually *fish for* them. Their meat is poor, and the roe is poisonous. They tear up your line with their needle-like teeth, they are extremely difficult to hook, and are treacherous to handle. And there has never been a more menacing-looking creature dragged from the murky depths.

But I will have to say, gar are a remarkable fish. They (and the freshwater bowfin [true mudfish]) have a primitive lung, which they have utilized since *before* the dinosaurs roamed our planet. In hot weather, when the water becomes anoxic, they can actually roll on the surface and gulp air, shortcutting the normal piscine practice of removing dissolved oxygen from the water with gills. And during the tremendous heat of the Mesozoic, this gave gar and bowfin a competitive edge, and ensured their survival for another quarter billion years.

Looking like a sleek, miniature gar is the **needlefish.** These fast minnow-eaters dart across the surface at great speed, and occasionally take hooks (they will grab shrimp), giving the fisherman quite a start. Cut up, their torso does make good bait.

There are two somewhat similar fish that are not great table fare, but are often caught along the docks and canals. **Pinfish** (locally called "piggy perch") are feisty little guys with small mouths but large appetites for shrimp. And although the large ones *may* be eaten, they excel as a bait for larger predators. I have caught tarpon by bouncing pinfish along the bottom of clear water on full moon nights, and nothing–and I mean NOTHING–is more exciting than a tarpon strike!

Between needlefish and pinfish, no shrimp is safe. There should be a study done to see how many hours of time are wasted fooling with these little marauders, zipping around and playing hide-and-seek, as they swipe expensive bait. But on dull days, they do keep us on "pins and needles." It should be said that there is another "piggy perch" often confused with pinfish, whose correct name is the **pigfish**. They are sometimes caught right along with pinfish.

There is excellent fishing in the deep waters off Galveston, and I encourage you to give this a try. It is a very different type of fishing and results are usually productive. Grouper may be taken in winter, and people frequently get their limit in a matter of hours. But in the warmer season, one can catch Kingfish, Snapper and Cobia (Ling or Ling Cod) out deep.

A few years ago, Texas enacted a controversial law to prohibit gill nets, fearing they severely cut populations of certain game fish species. Opinions on the effects of this vary with different sources, although those at Texas Parks and Wildlife firmly believe it aided fish populations. This did, however, put some people out of business, and certainly constituted a drastic measure. It has also been done in other states, such as Florida, as many felt populations of reds and others were diminishing due to these nets.

Needlefish

Regardless of "who's right" in this instance, the truth is, the ocean can't withstand the pressures our species place on it without some controls. The old notion that there is a limitless supply of fish is as outdated as the thinking that terrestrial populations of birds can't go extinct. If we make mistakes and overreact in an effort to conserve some of what we have for future generations, then these are mistakes we can forgive. But also, in fairness, let's not kid ourselves and think that sport-fishing doesn't take its toll on these species. There are over six times as many people on this planet as there were during the civil war. And our technology for catching fish is far more sophisticated as well. We all may be called on to sacrifice so that our grandchildren can take a rod down to the dock and bring back a few fish for supper.

Sharks are both a good example of a diminishing resource, as well as a creature many people don't care for. They are still caught in Galveston waters, mostly in the gulf. They will take dead meat readily, and sometimes live bait. Locally common species are the **Bull Shark, Bonnethead** (or "shovelnose"), and **Black-tipped**, but other species may be found, like **Hammerheads.**

Most people catch sharks and simply kill them, as their love for these ancient predators is about that of snakes. But sharks can be eaten, and they can also be released unharmed. Shark attacks (virtually always mistaken identity) are extremely rare; especially serious ones. At some point, we humans need to learn to live with our fellow inhabitants of this rock without feeling the compunction to kill everything that moves and cut down everything that grows.

Of course, now I have boxed myself into having to be benevolent to their cousins the **sting rays**! But really, there is no need to kill these (loathsome) creatures, either. Granted, they sometimes stab people wading in the surf, but can this honestly justify a death sentence for any and all sting rays that dare to bite our hooks? Despite having been nailed once by these despicable devils, I would suggest that we are capable of a kinder, gentler attitude toward even the lowly animals. One wonders if our species developing more respect for life could render our kind more peaceful to our own race. Life should be taken only with great care and consideration.

When walking in the waters around Galveston, try shuffling your feet. This scares off creatures like Blue Crabs (again, not my personal favorite!) and sting rays. Also, be aware of the times when there are sting ray migrations in progress (late spring and fall), and be **very** careful at night that the fish you are taking off your gig is actually a flounder!

In addition to rays, we have other depressed *Chondriicthes* called **skates.** These are much like rays, but have certain morphological differences. Possibly the most common skate is the **Clear-nosed Skate**, but we also have a few **Cow-nosed**, **Spotted** and occasionally tropical species. The skates are most famous for their egg cases, called "mermaid's purses." These are hard (like plastic), rectangular cases that are solid black and have hooks on each corner. This enables them to fasten on objects found at the bottom, where the eggs develop. Absent of this, they would bounce along the bottom (roller skate?) and wash up on shore destroying the eggs.

Many people wonder what the small fish around Galveston are, such as those found in the tidal creeks and canals. There are several common species, with vernacular names like mud minnow, mud fish, porgies, and so forth. One species found along the bayside shores is the **Long-nosed Killifish**. It is a couple of inches long, with black bars on the side and, yup, a long nose. They make very hardy bait, and are best hooked through the lips. There are other species of killifish, which some also call mollies. The Sheepshead Minnow is a short, fat creature with wide, light gray bands. It does less well on a hook, although frequently sold when little else is available.

For those interested in seeing fish in aquaria, Moody Gardens, located at Jones Road and 81st Street, is completing brand new tanks. In addition, they have an interesting rain forest display (with a few ill-chosen local animals mixed in), and some great movies that really bring nature to your feet. Also, Texas Parks and Wildlife has a nice facility called Sea Center on the far side of Brazosport (409) 292-0100.

42

The Fascinating World of Amphibians and Reptiles

These two cold-blooded classes of vertebrates have been with us for hundreds of millions of years, but are in a fight against extinction like they have never known. They have survived global floods, comets colliding with Earth, radiation bombardment, continental drift, ice ages, and many other threats which have exterminated other creatures. But today, they are disappearing at an alarming rate, and especially on Galveston Island. Here are some secrets about these two classes and one species of each found on the island.

Most amphibians easily suffer death through dessication, but toads have dry, warty skin that not only protects against salt and aridity, but predators as well. Our species is the Gulf Coast Toad, which is still relatively common in most parts of the island. Here is one showing adaptability in a remarkable way. He is not 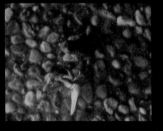 only camouflaging perfectly with the stones of a sidewalk, he is sitting by a dead fiddler crab eating insects which fly in to light on the carcass of the unfortunate crustacean. What a great idea!

Reptiles were once amphibians, but developed water-tight skin, claws, scales, and the ability to reproduce far from water. Many made lunch out of their amphibian ancestors!  But some, like these rattlesnakes, aid our species in predator control. Here, two rival males fight over a territory, but will not harm each other. Should we harm them?

CHAPTER 5: The
Herpetology of Galveston

There is no doubt that this island once held a tremendous population of reptiles and amphibians. With its forests, fields, wet areas and huge rat presence, snakes were likely everywhere. Lizards no doubt scurried all over the dry areas, and various frogs certainly made the night a noisy place. But unfortunately, there were no records kept, and the details of the island's past herpetology may never be known.

Today, as one would predict, there's little left of Galveston's herpefauna. Many of my snake records are multiple sightings of one individual and too often the record is of a snake found flattened on the road. That fate is most likely responsible, as is "development," for the serious decline in our cold-blooded vertebrates. But of what importance are a few scaly creatures to an island destined to become more and more populated with people in the 21st century?

The answer lies in the fact that this is an island. The life forms here that do not migrate to the mainland have been isolated on Galveston for thousands of years, and have begun the speciation process. The Ground Skinks are a perfect example. These diminutive lizards that some people mistakenly call "salamanders" may be seen in the moist woodlands, scurrying along the ground in search of tiny insects. They are found over the entire Eastern forest from Texas to the Atlantic and up to Canada.

Catch one, though, and compare it to one from the mainland. They are different; they have more striping on the side than mainland Ground Skinks. They are evolving due to geographic isolation, as there cannot be gene flow with the mainland. If they should disappear, a new species of lizard will go extinct before it ever develops. This scenario may have been played out with quite a few other species of reptiles, and we'll never even know they were diverging.

Indeed, island populations are fragile because islands are fragile ecosystems. The Great Storm of 1900 may well have completely altered the course of biosystems on the island, but these natural disasters are just that–natural–and acceptable. But the extermination of critical life forms cannot be justified simply in the name of "development." The wanton removal of forests and the hideous filling of wetlands (I've watched it happen) rob future generations of organisms we may never know of; all in the name of money.

So, what is left in any kind of numbers? By my research, there are about a half-dozen species each of snakes, lizards, turtles and frogs. Other species that are either extirpated from the island, or are on an irreversible fast track to disappearing, will be mentioned separately.

Amphibians found on Galveston include five species of frogs and toads. Given the vocal nature of these creatures, it seems unlikely there are other species unrecorded. Plus, given the place of these creatures low on the food chain, there really needs to be a fairly stable population, or the species would disappear. But these five, for the moment, are surviving.

The **Gulf Coast Toad** is found throughout the island in sandy areas, where it emerges at night to get its share of the island's insect population. Even surviving in the city, they are widespread and familiar to residents. But though they are well-adapted to the island's dry habitat, their nature as amphibians requires fresh water in which to breed. And in the latter part of the twentieth century, fresh water became in short supply. From drought to development, water disappearing spells certain doom for any amphibian attempting to eke out a living.

As a species, the Gulf Coast Toad is an interesting creature. It possesses paratoid glands on the back of the head which contain a noxious, milky substance. Extremely bitter to the taste, many animals find out the hard way that toads don't taste good. Moreover, when attacked, toads puff up full of air and this disgusting mass of warts and white goo hardly looks like a meal for would-be attackers. There is, however, a small population of hog-nosed snakes on the island, and their preferred lunch is these hapless creatures.

Toads are clearly beneficial in that they control many insect pests, and will flourish where freshwater breeding ponds exist. They also make good pets for kids, and eat small bugs and such in a terrarium. But watch for them on warm nights while driving in the neighborhoods, as tires seem impervious to any kind of noxious chemical and puffing-up creature.

Another creature with the "toad" name is the **Narrow-mouthed Toad.** It is hardly a real toad as it has smooth skin, a tiny head with no paratoid glands, and prefers damp areas. It is actually unrelated to conventional groups such as toads, true frogs and treefrogs. It has managed to survive the salt and stressful conditions thus far, and with a place to breed, might continue.

Narrow-mouthed Toads are tiny blackish creatures that are most often found under boards, logs and other debris on the island. Their shape is unmistakable, with a fat body and almost no head! Their nasal call is equally bizarre, as it sounds for all the world like a Norelco razor. This call is given as breeding time nears, and can get a little hard on the ears.

These creatures, which range over much of the East, are very susceptible to predation, cars (in the breeding season) and drought. Preserving as much of the island's wetlands as possible will ensure a fighting chance to these delicate, unique creatures.

Grabbing a foothold where they may not have originally lived is the **Bullfrog.** These big, bulky predators reproduce successfully in shallow ponds and live along their edges. Their main food seems to be dragonflies, which they lunge for off their enormous, muscular hind legs. But when summer ends, the diet becomes more complicated. Once, in an amazing few seconds, I videoed a male Bullfrog actually catch and devour a Red-breasted Nuthatch on the fence at my pond!

Bullfrogs are mottled with green and brown, and are virtually unmistakable. Their bulbous eyes on their wide head give them a mystical look, and their ability to camouflage is remarkable. In my experience, there are no other true frogs (genus Rana) on the island, so they have exploited this niche to the fullest. As is so often the case, though, it is the introduced organisms that thrive while the native species struggle to exist. Where Bullfrogs cross paths with smaller, native species of frogs and toads, all that will be left are fat Bullfrogs.

Treefrogs are adapted for life in the canopy, but are mostly seen on windows in wet and warm weather. The common species on the island is the **Squirrel Treefrog**. It is little more than an inch long, and is highly variable in color. Most specimens are greenish or brownish, but may be gray in the island's sandy environment. Their calls sound like the barking of squirrels, thus the name. In the warm months, they will gather at any wetland left on the island, to lay and fertilize eggs. Their reproductive success is important, though, as they are eaten by an amazing assortment of predators, including birds, snakes, mammals (including feral cats) and larger frogs.

Also found on the island in modest numbers is the larger **Green Treefrog**. It has a bold light line down the side, making it easily distinguishable from the above species. Greens issue a honking sound in wet weather, and seem to prefer marshes more than Squirrel Treefrogs. This may be why they are uncommon on the island, as Galveston has few real freshwater marshes left. This is a species which could disappear off the island, and their honking on summer nights would be missed.

Amphibians are in trouble on a worldwide basis. Even in places where the impact of humans is minimal, species are disappearing at an alarming rate. Because of the fragile ecosystem of Galveston Island, the amount of stress (such as salt present), an abundance of natural and unnatural predators and Lord knows what else, we could lose our resident amphibians in a few short years. The best plan for preservation is to preserve our existing wetlands and avoid harmful insecticides. Absent that, warm nights without frog calls will be as sad as Rachel Carson's Silent Spring.

Reptiles are in little better shape on the island, and we have, in fact, been losing more species of snakes than all amphibians that have occurred here. Traffic, deforestation and predators such as feral cats, coupled with man's dislike for snakes, may have cost us more species than the meager half dozen or so we have left. Lizards have hardly fared better, with some gone and others just hanging on. First though, let's see what Galveston does have.

Snakes are still represented on Galveston Island in small numbers in some of the more natural areas. Of these, two are poisonous, and should be watched for. Both are pit vipers, and although the chance of a bite being fatal in this day and age is slight, neither bite should be taken as anything less than a serious injury.

Snakebite treatment has changed radically from the old cut and suck, use ice, and give him some brandy approach. In today's world of modern medicine, the most important step for treating a snakebite is to ***get the victim to the hospital*** as soon as possible. There is no need to go into the problems associated with the outdated remedies listed above, but suffice it to say antivenom is a powerful medicine that greatly reduces the chance of death, as well as tissue loss. Anything one does that delays the administration of this serum is detrimental to the victim.

The **Cottonmouth**, known in the vernacular as a water moccasin, is not an uncommon snake on Galveston Island. It is a heavy-bodied, mostly brownish-black snake, with significant black on the rear of the snake. It holds its head up high, and opens its mouth in readiness to bite. When they are stopped and coil up, they will vibrate their tails like a rattlesnake without the rattle. A field mark that seals the identification is the black stripe down the side of the face, camouflaging the eye, that forms a "mask." But truthfully, in the absence of any freshwater, nonpoisonous "watersnakes," on the island, any snake here that looks like a cottonmouth probably is one! Cottonmouths are partial to wet areas, but venture into woods and grassy areas unflinchingly.

The Laffite's Cove Nature Preserve is crawling with them, especially in the fall, but they can be found regularly any place west of the city. They often "stand their ground" because they "think" they are hidden, but will bite if stepped on. And though their bite is not as serious as a rattler, a great deal of tissue loss can result, as well as a re-write on your book of pain.

Cottonmouths eat a variety of vertebrate foods from fish, frogs and other reptiles, to rats and birds. In fact, there isn't much that doesn't interest these opportunistic gluttons. It is painful to me that on the island, they probably eat more migrant birds than anything, but let's just let nature take her course. Aside from their ugly appearance, and a demeanor to match, they are a marvelous work of evolution, and may be more adaptable than any snake in America.

The **Western Diamond-backed Rattlesnake** still roams the wilder areas of the island, and may occasionally be seen amongst the dunes of the west end – thus a call for caution. Shy snakes, they "pay rent" by the enormous numbers of rats they eat, and give people plenty of warning when the two meet. Sadly, they are probably doomed to disappear off the island; this handsome snake is one more example of humans not being able to get along with our fellow inhabitants of earth.

Few experiences in nature draw our complete attention more than meeting a rattlesnake on its terms. The rattle begins the deafening buzz, and the head and neck begin to rise, like a huge arm studded with so many diamonds. Not swerving in its attention, the head keeps its constant vigil on our lower torso, which is probably too close to the compact coils for our own good. It's a moment frozen in time that acts as a decisive measure of our attitude toward nature: Do we kill it, or just admire it from a safe distance and let it live out its magnificent life? If it's out in the wilderness where it belongs, I submit we grow as a species every time we opt to let it live. And by the way, the *vast* majority of snakebites occur *after* the person has seen the snake–usually in a misguided attempt to catch or kill the beast. Live and let live!

One of the great snakes in our country is still found in modest numbers on Galveston: **Speckled Kingsnake**. This shiny, handsome snake is not only harmless, it can hardly be convinced to bite. But underneath this friendly exterior lurks a courageous snake that will kill and eat poisonous snakes. It is immune to the venom of our native pit vipers, and is probably an agent of population control at least on our cottonmouths, if not rattlesnakes.

Speckled Kingsnakes are a basic iridescent shiny black, with yellowing spots over their entire body. They have smooth scales, unlike the rough, keeled scales of the pit vipers above. They are generally seen crossing roads and paths, and are somewhat fond of wet areas. Here they can look for turtle eggs and other snakes that have come to drink. Probably the lion's share of their diet is also the same rats that feed other snakes, owls, hawks, kites, coyotes, and rat traps.

The **Gulf Coast Ribbon Snake** is a slender, harmless creature with yellow and black stripes running *down* the length of the snake. It loves grassy areas around water, where it consumes small frogs and minnows. Called "grass snakes" by many, ribbon snakes wander into yards, and constitute one species that is hard to accuse of being poisonous. Both kingsnakes and ribbon snakes are diurnal, being found more by day than at night.

Possibly the most numerous snake on the island may be the least familiar. The **Gulf Salt Marsh Snake** is an abundant resident in the salt marshes all over the island, but hides well in the cordgrass and needlerush. It is a harmless snake, and our only representative of the huge group of watersnakes so abundant in the rest of East Texas and Eastern North America.

Salt marsh snakes are black and white streaked, so they mimic grass stalks when still. They are usually at the edge of tidal creeks, trying to grab small fish that swim by. Armed with a good set of teeth, they take their quarry to the shore and swallow it head first and whole–like all snakes. If captured they will make some attempt to bite initially, but soon calm down and can be handled with relative ease. I do not recommend them for long-term pets. I would also make a plea not to remove other nonpoisonous snakes from the island's ecosystem, as we need all the breeding stock there is. Snakes are too common on the mainland to risk impacting such a fragile area, and many species from elsewhere may be bought fairly cheaply in pet shops.

There are several other species of snakes–all harmless–that I know of from one or two records, and which seem on the verge of extirpation on Galveston. Most records are from road kills, which is the primary reason they may disappear. This list, which may be incomplete, follows:

Rough Earth Snake, Eastern Garter Snake, Rough Green Snake, hog-nosed snake (species?), Western Coachwhip, Yellow-bellied Racer, and Texas Rat Snake. For those who wonder, I am aware of no records of copperheads on the island, but can say it is one of the most misidentified creatures (not) known to man. Frankly, I do not believe most people exercise caution in identifications of snakes—especially potentially poisonous ones–just as I do not trust many "snake stories."

Lizards are hardly more common than snakes on Galveston, and awfully secretive as well. It is a little curious that they are not better represented, but at least one expert hypothesizes that periodic hurricanes will diminish the populations of lizards and other small creatures on islands. It is very likely that no wild animal is killed by feral cats more than lizards, and I find it in the realm of possibility that cats are a chief reason lizards are not flourishing on Galveston Island.

Found all over the island in small numbers where trees and bushes are present are **Green Anoles**. These are the "chameleons" that change color, and extend their reddish throat fan as a territorial display (true chameleons are Old World creatures). Their most common colors seem to be green and brown, generally a solid of either. This is often due to whether they are on leaves or bark, but this may not be the whole story.

Anoles are fun (and harmless) for kids to play with, and make good pets. They are probably quite beneficial in insect control, and provide a food source for some migrating birds like cuckoos. In some areas (like Florida) they have been out-competed by introduced species of anoles, but here they seem to be a stable, though not thriving population.

Ground Skinks are abundant little creatures of woodlands and border grass. They are brown, and look like a salamander scurrying along the ground. As mentioned previously, they may constitute a separate subspecies, and further research is indicated. They eat small insects, and are as benign as a creature can be.

Geckos are small nocturnal lizards from other parts of the world that have colonized the city of Galveston. They have slit pupils and toes adapted for climbing on smooth surfaces. Many residents have probably seen these light gray lizards on their walls and window panes, and wondered what they were. They are quite harmless, and probably eat a lot of insects.

In some of the island's drier areas, the **Six-lined Racerunner** still lives. It is an extremely fleet reptile, with bold stripes running lengthwise down its back. In an amazing factoid, racerunners have even been known to run *on their hind legs,* when hurried by a predator or approaching car. They walk in a jerky motion, extending their tongue frequently. A good place to see this species is on the south side of the walkway into the woods at Laffite's Cove Nature Preserve when it is warm weather.

Appearing like a snake is the **Slender Glass Lizard**. Lacking legs, it can be identified as a lizard by its blunt teeth, ear opening, movable eye lid, dorsolateral fold, and tail that is made to break off. These lizards may be sandy or tan colored, and have dark stripes running *down* the body. They have a rather small, pointed head, like other lizards. Glass lizards seem to prefer grassy areas, and are sometimes seen in my Indian Beach neighborhood. They relish grasshoppers, but captive ones don't always eat well.

Texas Horned Lizards (horny toads) are subjects of great concern among conservationists in our state. They have disappeared at an alarming rate, due to habitat loss, highways and fire ants. On Galveston, they were common at one time, but have all but vanished in recent years. One of the truly unique reptiles, horned lizards sport protective "horns," have incredible camouflage with their depressed bodies, and can shoot blood out of their eyes as a defense. Any person locating a site with horned lizards *anywhere* in Texas should contact Texas Parks and Wildlife immediately.

Turtles are predominately represented on Galveston Island by one species, **Red-eared Turtle**. It is confined to ponds and other freshwater wetlands, though their population has diminished in the past few years. These "sliders" sun themselves on logs and the bank, *sliding* off into the safety of the water at the slightest sign of danger. Ponds along Stewart Road may offer the best glimpses of this omnivore. Occasionally, they are seen crossing the road, and good Samaritans often stop to help them across. Keeping them as pets is unwise, as their population is rather unstable, and they do bite painfully!

I am aware of other species of turtles which are all but extirpated on Galveston. This list might include the box turtle and mud turtle; possibly others. But on our beaches occasionally crawl sea turtles such as the **Ridley** or the **Loggerhead**. If one of these is discovered, please contact the stranded turtle network through Texas A&M at (409) 766-3525.

The last reptile in our list is the largest, the **American Alligator**. Not a common visitor, 'gators occasionally show up in canals and swimming pools just to give the locals a scare. Texas seems to have a rather sensational view of these ancient beasts that watched the dinosaurs come and go. Everyone seems sure they lay in wait, ready to grab the first unsuspecting human victim they can find. (Note: this is written by a Florida boy who grew up swimming with alligators!) In actuality, they are shy, retiring creatures who are far more scared of us than we are of them. But one must bear in mind that alligators have the smallest brain for their body mass of any vertebrate, so associating humans with food (when we have unwisely fed them) is a natural sequence of events. And anything as powerful as an alligator with a brain so tiny is a pretty scarey thing. By the way, there are no **crocodiles** on the entire Gulf coast.

No group of animals on the island needs our help more than the reptiles and amphibians. We've taken their forests, filled in their wet areas, beat and shot them, run over them with our cars and unleashed mortal (feline) enemies on them. This just isn't right! For us to hold on to some of our island's biodiversity, we must change our attitudes and co-exist with scaly and slimy creatures. We must lose our prejudices or lose a dozen species that were here long before the first boat full of Galvestonians rowed to shore. Please, give these animals a break!

List of Plates

Primitive Marine Animals

Plate 1

Man of War

Sea Anemone

Cannonball

Chiton

Periwinkle

Cockle

Quahog

Octopus

Plate 2   Echinoderms and Arthropods

Sea Cucumber

Brittlestar

Starfish

Sea Urchin

Shrimp

Blue Crab

Hermit Crabs

Stone Crab

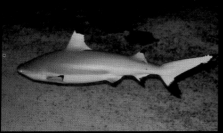

Blacktip Shark

Bull Shark

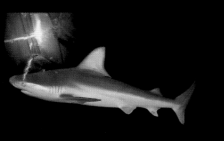

Sand Shark

Nurse Shark

Skate Egg Case

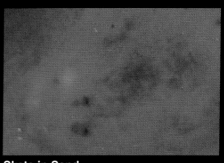

Skate in Sand

Stingray

Sea Catfish

Plate 4
Common Galveston Fish

Red Drum

Flounder

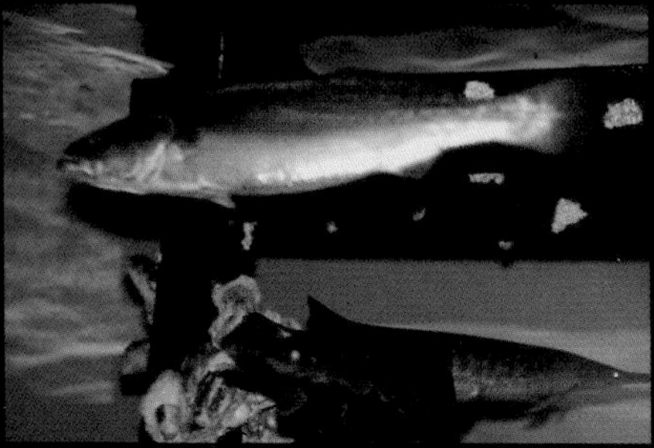

Trout and Gar

Black Drum

Pinfish

Sheepshead Minnow

Baby Mullet

Long-Nosed Killifish

Frogs and Turtles

Plate 5

Narrow-Mouthed Toad

Bullfrog

Squirrel Treefrog

Green Treefrog

Box Turtle

Common Snapping Turtle

Mud Turtle

Red-Eared Turtle

Plate 6

Snakes of the Island

Western Cottonmouth

Western Diamond-backed Rattlesnake

Western Coachwhip

Yellow-bellied Racer

Speckled Kingsnake

Texas Rat Snake

Gulf Salt Marsh Snake

Gulf Coast Ribbon Snake

Green Anoles mating

Green Anole (Brown)

Ground Skink

Gecko

Six-lined Racerunner

Texas Horned Lizard

Slender Glass Lizard

Alligator

Plate 8   Mammals

Armadillo

Raccoon

Opossum

Coyote

Cotttontail Rabbit

Cotton Rat

Gray Squirrel

Fox Squirrel

Hawks of Galveston

Plate 9

Red-tailed Hawk

Red-shouldered Hawk

Broad-winged Hawk (adult)

Broad-winged Hawk (immature)

Nothern Harrier

Swainson's Hawk

Sharp-shinned Hawk

Cooper's Hawk

Black Vulture

Turkey Vulture

Caracara

Osprey

Peregrine

American Kestrel

White-tailed Kite

Merlin

Owls and Doves

Plate 11

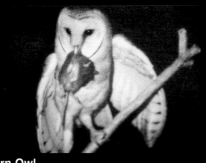

Barn Owl

Great Horned Owl

Mourning Dove

Collared Dove

Rock Doves

Ground Dove

nca Dove

White-winged Dove

Plate 12

Woodpeckers and other Birds

Red-bellied Woodpecker

Northen Flicker

Yelllow-bellied Sapsucker

Downy Woodpecker

Eastern Phoebe

Horned Lark

Purple Martin

Blue Jay

Wrens, Mimic Thrushes, etc.

Plate 13

Carolina Wren

House Wren

Marsh Wren

Sedge Wren

Northern Mockingbird

Brown Thrasher

Gray Catbird

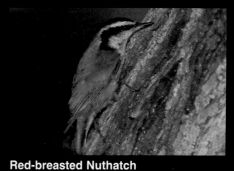

Red-breasted Nuthatch

Plate 14

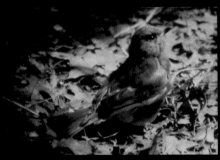

Eastern Bluebird

Cedar Waxwing

American Robin

Brown Creeper

Hermit Thrush

Loggerhead Shrike

American Pipit

Blue-gray Gratcatcher

Black and White Warbler (female)

Orange-crowned Warbler

Pine Warbler (male)

Yellow-rumped Warbler

Palm Warbler

Yellow-throated Warbler

Common Yellowthroat (male)

Common Yellowthroat (female)

Ruby-crowned Kinglet (male)

Golden-crowned Kinglet (male)

Plate 16
Finches, etc.

Northern Cardinal (male)

Northern Cardinal (female)

American Goldfinch (male)

American Goldfinch (female)

House Sparrow (male)

House Sparrow (female)

Bobolink

Eastern Meadowlark

Lincoln's Sparrow

Clay-colored Sparrow

Savannah Sparrow

Seaside Sparrow

Song Sparrow

Swamp Sparrow

White-crowned Sparrow

White-throated Sparrow

Plate 18

Blackbirds

Boat-tailed Grackle

Great-tailed Grackles

Common Grackle

European Starling

Brewer's Blackbird

Brown-headed Cowbird

Red-winged Blackbird

Red-winged Blackbird (f)

Common Loon (breeding)

Common Loons (winter)

Red-throated Loon (winter)

Pacific Loon (winter)

Eared Grebe (winter)

Pied-billed Grebe (winter)

Black Skimmers nesting

Black Skimmer feeding

Plate 20

Pelicans and Allies

Brown Pelican (adult)

Brown Pelican (immature)

Brown and White Pelicans

Brown Pelicans diving

Northern Gannnet landing

Northern Gannet (intermediate)

Magnificent Frigatebird (male)

Both cormorant species

Great Blue Heron

Great Blue Heron flying

Reddish Egret (dark phase)

Reddish Egret (immature)

Tri-colored Heron

Litttle Blue Heron

Green Heron

Sandhill Cranes

Plate 22

Snowy Egret

Great Egret

Cattle Egret (breeding)

Reddish Egret (white phase)

Little Blue Heron (immature)

White Ibis

Roseate Spoonbill (immature)

Wood Stork

Brown Waders

Plate 23

Black-crowned Night Heron (adult)

Yellow-crowned Night Heron (adult)

Black-crowned Night Heron (immature)

Yellow-crowned Night Heron (immature)

Least Bittern

American Bittern

White-faced Ibis

White Ibis (immature)

Plate 24

Freshwater Ducks

Blue-winged Teal mating

Green-winged Teal

Mottled Ducks

Both Whistling-ducks

Mallards

Gadwall

Northern Shoveler

Northern Pintail

Geese and Diving Ducks

Plate 25

Snow Geese (both forms)

Snow Geese flying

Am. Wigeon and Lesser Scaup (male)

Ruddy Duck (male)

American Goldeneye (male)

Bufflehead (male)

Ring-necked Duck

Red-breasted Mergansers

Plate 26

Rails of Galveston

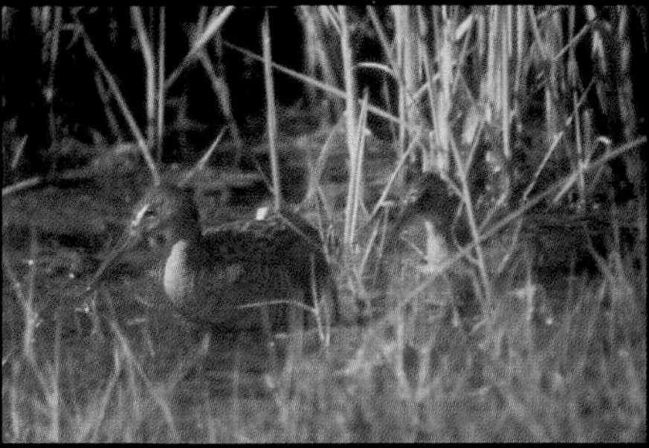

Clapper Rail

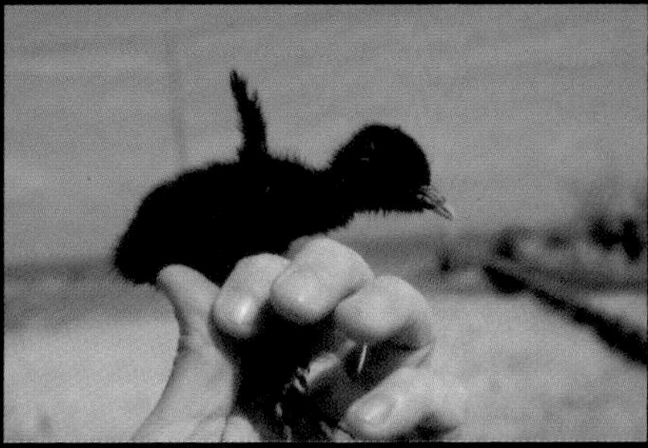

Clapper Rail (chick)

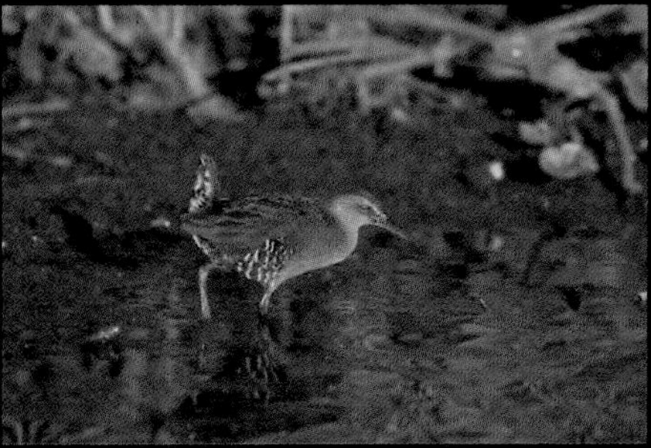

Viginia Rail

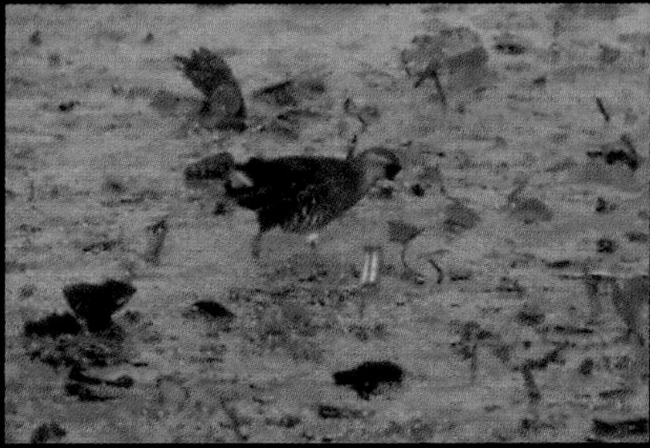

Sora

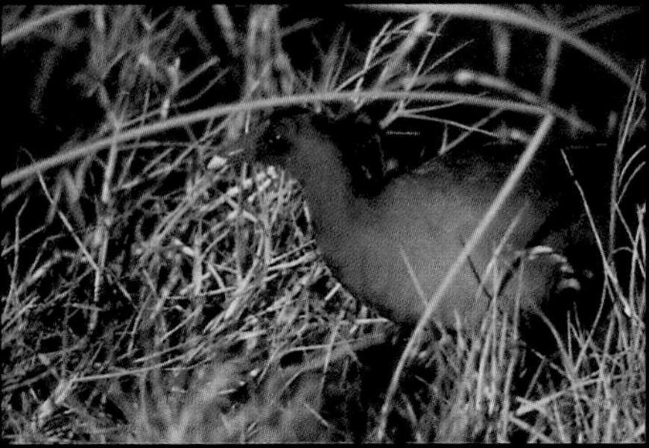

Common Moorhem

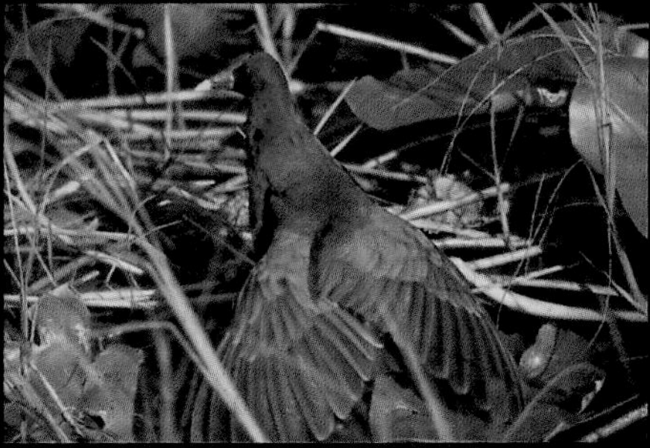

Puple Gallinule

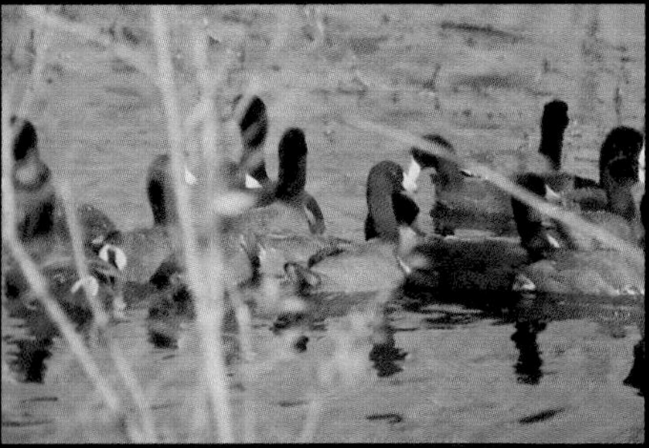

American Coots

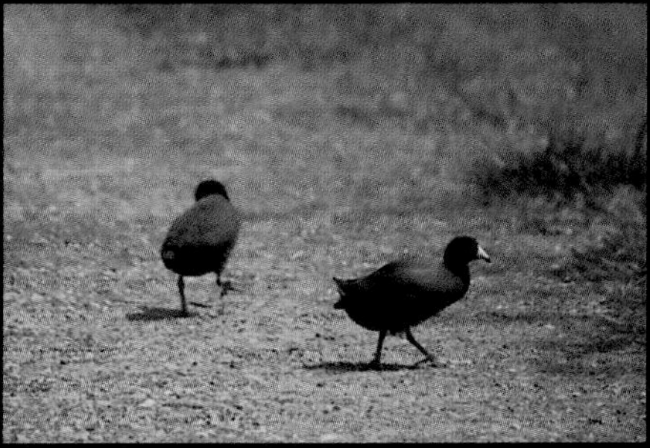

American Coots

Killdeer

Killdeer nest

Wilson's Plover

Semipalmated Plover

Snowy Plover

Piping Plover

Golden Plover (breeding)

Golden Plover (winter)

American Oystercatcher

Black-necked Stilt

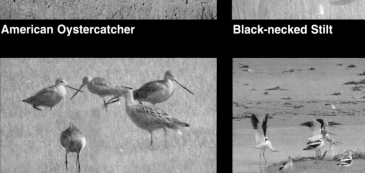

Marbled Godwit and Long-billed Curlew

American Avocets (both plumages)

Whimbrel (winter)

Upland Sandpiper

Greater Yellowlegs

Lesser Yellowlegs

Medium and Small Sandpipers

Plate 29

Solitary Sandpiper

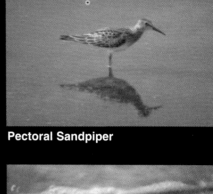

Pectoral Sandpiper

Buff-breasted Sandpiper

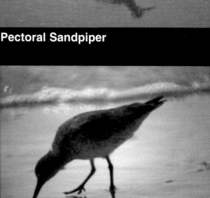

Red Knot (winter)

Western Sandpiper (breeding)

Semipalmated Sandpiper (winter)

Least Sandpiper (winter)

White-rumped Sandpiper (winter)

Plate 30

Ruddy Turnstones (winter& breeding)

Spotted Sandpiper (breeding)

Common Snipe

Wilson's Phalarope (breeding)

Long-billed Dowitcher (breeding)

Long-billed Dowitcher and Sanderling

Stilt Sandpiper

Dunlin (breeding)

Laughing Gulls (breeding)

Laughing Gull (winter)

Herring Gulls (3 plumages)

Laughing and Franklin's Gulls

Ring-billed Gill (adult)

Ring-billed Gull (immature)

Ionaparte's Gulls feeding

Herring Gull (immature)

Plate 32

Our Island's Terns

Forster's Tern (adult)

Caspian and Royal Terns

Common Tern (breeding)

Common Tern (winter)

Gull-billed Tern

Black Terns (ad & im) behind Skimmer

Sandwich Tern

Least Terns courting

Chuck-will's Widow

Common Nighthawk and chick

Whip-poor-will

Groove-billed Ani

Yellow-billed Cuckoo

Black-billed Cuckoo

Ruby-throated Hummingbird (m)

Chimney Swift

Barn Swallow

Cliff Swallow (at nest)

Plate 34

Vermillion Flycatcher

Western Kingbird

Scissor-tailed Flycatcher

Great-crested Flycatcher

Acadian Flycatcher

Eastern Wood Pewee

Least Flycatcher

Yellow-bellied Flycatcher

Alder Flycatcher

Willow Flycatcher

Gray-cheeked Thrush

Swainson's Thrush

Veery

Wood Thrush

Red-eyed Vireo

White-eyed Vireo

Yellow-throated Vireo

Blue-headed Vireo

Warbling Vireo

Philadelphia Vireo

Plate 36

Warblers

Black-throated Green W. (male)

Yellow Warbler (male)

Golden-winged Warbler (male)

Magnolia Warbler (male)

Blue-winged Warbler (male)

Tennessee Warbler (male)

Chestnut-sided Warbler (male)

Cape May Warbler (male)

Black-throated Blue W. (male)

Nashville Warbler (male)

Canada Warbler (male)

Hooded Warbler (male)

Louisiana Waterthrush (male)

Northern Waterthrush (male)

Kentucky Warbler (male)

Ovenbird (male)

American Redstart (male)

Prothonotary Warbler (male)

Plate 38

Warblers III

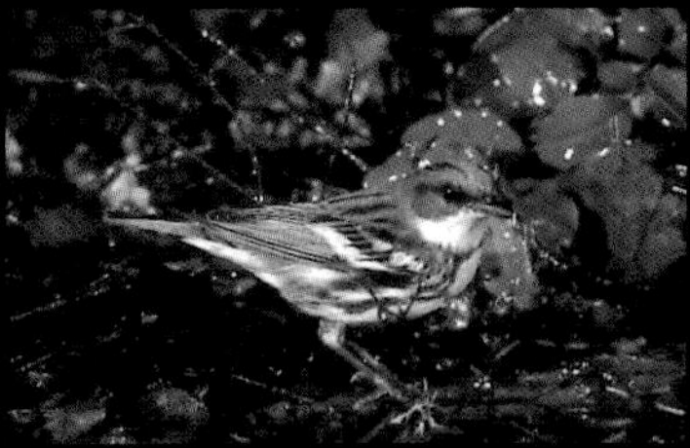

Cerulean Warbler (male)

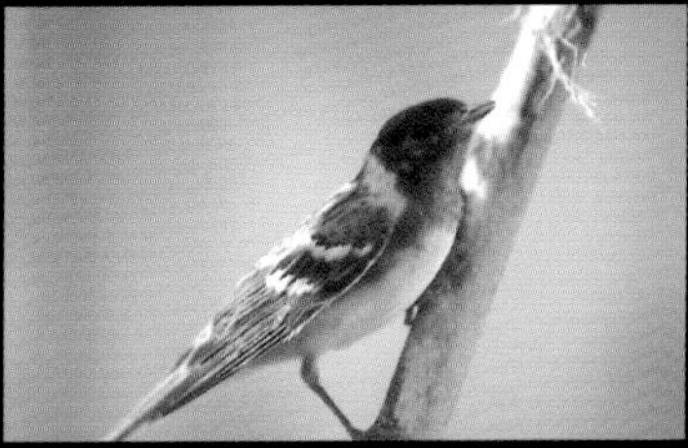

Bay-breasted Warbler (male)

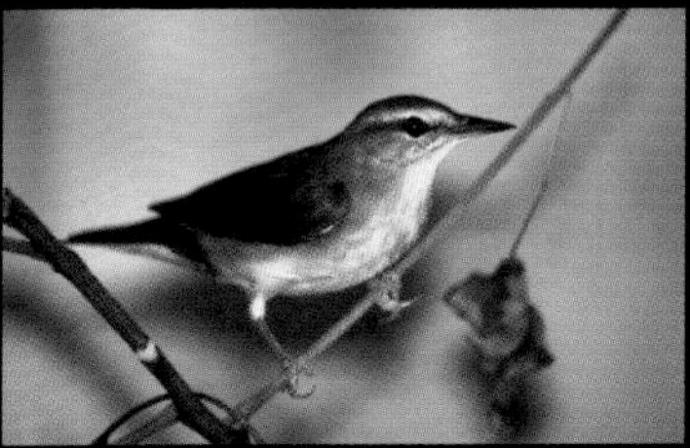

Swainson's Warbler (male)

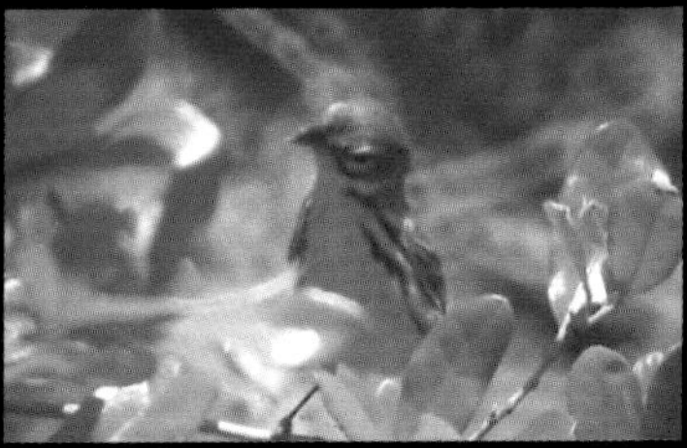

Prairie Warbler (male)

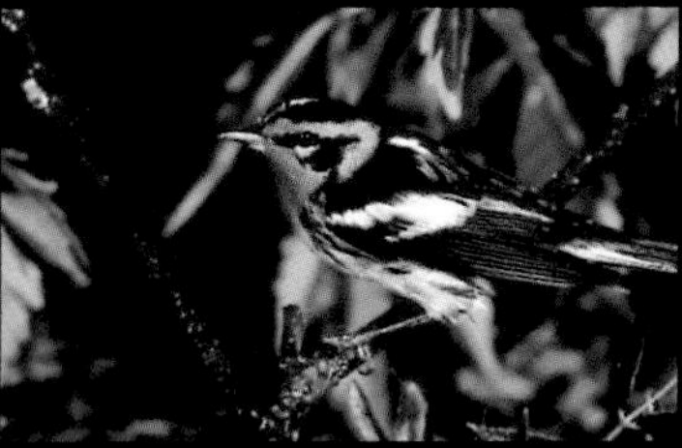

Blackburnian Warbler (male)

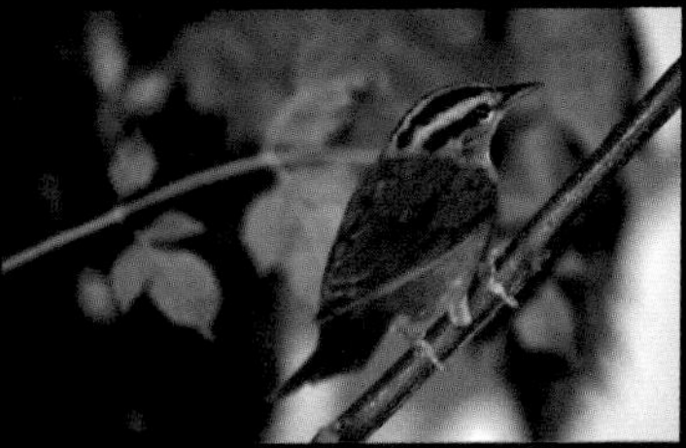

Worm-eating Warbler (male)

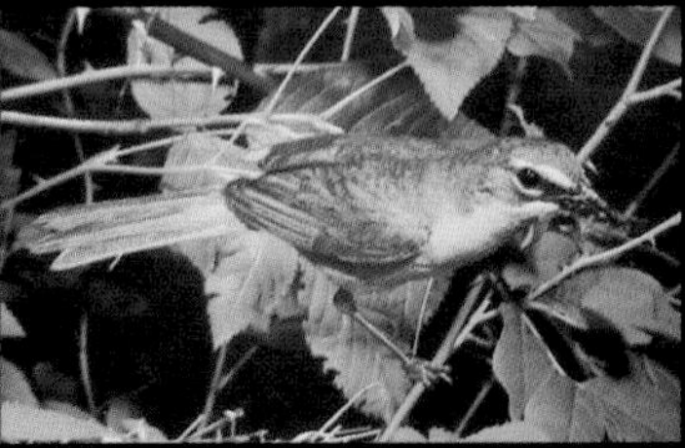

Yellow-breasted Chat (male)

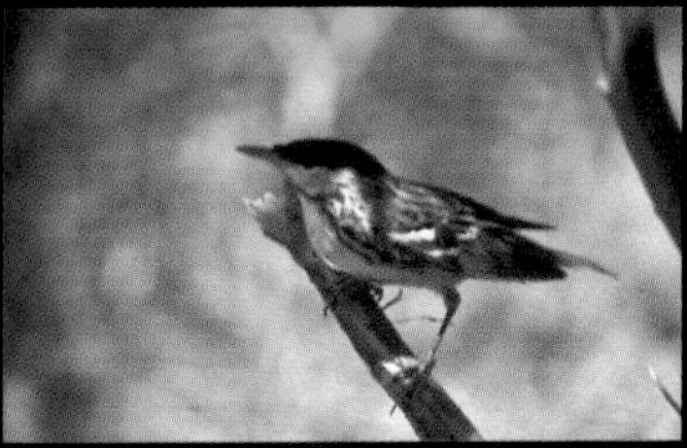

Blackpoll Warbler (male)

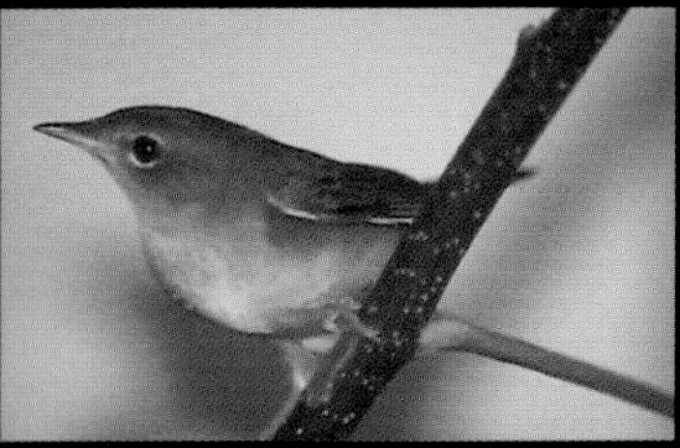

Mourning Warbler (female)

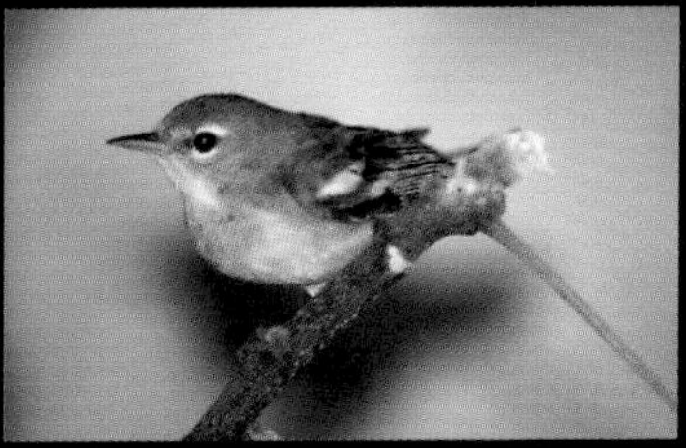

Northern Parula (female)

Baltimore Oriole (male)

Orchard Oriole (male)

Baltimore Oriole (female)

Orchard Oriole (female)

Summer Tanager (male)

Summer Tanager (female)

Scarlet Tanager (male)

Scarlet Tanager (female)

Dickcissel (male)

Dickcissel (female)

Plate 40

Migrant Finches, etc.

Indigo Bunting (male)

Indigo Bunting (female)

Painted Bunting (male)

Painted Bunting (female)

Blue Grosbeak (male)

Blue Grosbeak (female)

Rose-breasted Grosbeak (male)

Rose-breasted Grosbeak (female)

Yellow-headed Blackbird (male)

Bobolink (male)

CHAPTER **6: Our Mammalian Cousins**

As the forests on Galveston Island continue to disappear, so do many of the mammals that have historically inhabited the island. Many of the common creatures we know from other parts of the South are present here, and are still seen on occasion–especially west of the city.

There are many mammals that can safely be listed as *not* occurring on the island. Among them are deer, skunk, shrew, feral hog, bear, wolf, weasel, mountain lion, ground squirrel, prairie dogs or otter (though the occasional stray is possible). There are probably no bobcats or foxes left, nor Swamp Rabbits. Mammals can be secretive, though, so its best not to be dogmatic.

__Bats__ are uncommon on Galveston, and are little more than insectivorous mice on wings. They are occasionally seen, and the most likely species is the **Eastern Yellow Bat.** Identification in the air is quite difficult, though, as there are few field marks, and size can be tricky. Other species to look for include **Seminole Bat** (in the areas with more trees), **Eastern Pipistrel** (in more open areas) and possibly a **Big Brown Bat.** Other migrating species are possible.

Bats should not be feared. They are valuable for eating bugs, though their primary diet seems to be the more innocuous beetles. Incidents of rabies in bats are far more rare than commonly believed, and they'll only bite people if handled. In fact, some couldn't even penetrate our skin.

Eastern Yellow Bat

Probably the most abundant mammal found out here is the **Cotton Rat.** They scurry around all over the scrub and grasslands, eating various vegetable matter. By their sheer numbers, they provide a tremendous food source for many predators such as rattlesnakes and kingsnakes, and raptors such as White-tailed Kites, Red-tailed Hawks (in winter) and Northern Harriers. There are some other mammals that probably eat rats, as well.

Cotton Rats are the "wild" rat of the island. They are not generally found in the city and do not carry diseases. They are shy creatures and want no quarrel with humans. Their larger cousins, the **Black Rat and Norway Rat**, are the "domestic" rats of urban areas, told from Cotton Rats by their long tails. I am unaware of any true mice on the island, but they probably occur.

Blacks and Norways are introduced from Europe–like pigeons, starlings and House Sparrows– and create all kinds of havoc for our kind. They tear up houses, spread germs, scurry around in our attics, and chew wires and important cords in half. They're intelligent, adaptable, and royal pains in the derriere. The cute, benign, white lab rat we all know is but a shadow of the real members of this pair of alien species, which has actually *killed* human babies in this state! Fortunately, they are quite susceptible to rat poison and rat traps and may be controlled with some effort.

Gray and Fox Squirrels survive between cars, cats and BB guns in town, feasting on the island's prolific supply of acorns. The larger fox squirrels, found southwest of Galveston on the mainland, only rarely occur here, though an ancestral population probably existed. As few areas where they inhabit will support new oak trees, they probably have little effect on the environment in the city and peoples' yards. But they are friendly, interesting creatures which may lure a beautiful Red-tailed Hawk into our neighborhoods for the occasional lesson on predation.

Raccoons remain regular west of Galveston, though they are less prone to visit within the city than some other wild mammals. They feed on low tide flats and crayfish in the ditches, but are so adaptable that they can find a living about anywhere. Today, rabid 'coons are quite rare, but a very tame one should be avoided. Raccoons are omnivores, munching on the island's bounty of berries and other vegetable material to supplement their taste for crustaceans.

Opossums may be found right in town and are common west of Galveston. These omnivores forage at night most of the time and sleep by day. They're quite adaptable little creatures, even climbing up on our windows at night, taking dragon flies off the panes. Their prehensile, bare tail, whitish coat and low-slung head make them unmistakable.

Possums are our only marsupials in this continent, with young being born so small, a teaspoon could hold two or three. But they survive against all odds in many places, and escape by playing dead when really in trouble. But their greatest story is how they got to America–not on cattle boats or through other unwitting or intentional means of man. They crossed over the Antarctic from Australia when the icy continent was high in latitude (and not so cold). Then on to South America when Tierra del Fuego later articulated to Antarctica, and up South America to the north tip of present-day Colombia, and into Central America in the Miocene when it finally connected at present-day Panama. What a voyage!

The **armadillo** is still found in small numbers across the island, modestly probing around for insects and tubers underground. Its remarkable shell renders it impervious to many enemies, but cars still take their toll on these gentle but dimwitted creatures. This is a species I predict will disappear off Galveston in the next few years, simply through collisions with automobiles.

One many of us wish had never made it to Galveston is the **nutria.** A South American native, the nutria was more valuable feeding anacondas in Venezuela than eating our gardens and driving our dogs crazy. A rather aquatic animal, nutrias are usually found in close proximity of ponds, canals and marshes, waddling along like a miniature beaver. Today, they are fully established and acclimated to people–sometimes seen in family groups along the roadside. Some residents use "gopher bait" to eliminate them from melon patches, etc., but caution should be exercised when applying any poison to the environment.

I am aware of at least one **beaver** that spent a few destructive weeks on Galveston Island. At the Laffitte's Cove Nature Preserve, it ate about every small tree it could get its massive incisors on and finally disappeared. On an island which hardly needs forces other than developers taking down trees, we can hope the beavers never take too much of a liking to our wood.

Cottontail rabbits are found in some of the more protected areas of the island and are often an easy sighting at the Preserve. Their population is irruptive, and some spring it seems they are quite a common creature west of the city. With all the Red-tailed Hawks, coyotes and feral cats in the area, they face a perilous existence. Swamp Rabbits do not seem to occur here, though they should be looked for around some of the damp areas of the island.

Coyotes exist in small numbers on Galveston Island, such as right next to my house. These live in an (illegal) trash dump my neighbor maintains, and I only hear them when sirens go by. I've just seen one once, early in the morning when I happened to be up on my sky deck. They are exceedingly shy creatures, and create no problems of which I am aware. They probably feed on Cotton Rats for the most part, but may also take a wide range of other animals. Hopefully, they have an appetite for feral cats as well. With their habits being what they are, surviving in such a low population, inbreeding may be their greatest enemy.

Of very serious concern to any ecologist, or persons caring about defenseless animals, is the rise in numbers of **feral cats**. These "domestic cats turned wild" inhabit many places on the island, from a population on the jetties at Seawall and 61st, to garbage dumps and scattered individuals on the prowl. They, and their fully domestic friends (still owned by people), do enormous damage to small snakes, wild rats, lizards, many invertebrates, and *especially* birds. These innocent animals have no idea what a cat is, so they easily fall victim.

Aside from the ecological damage, turning a cat out is probably the cruelest thing one could do. They soon contract horrible diseases and suffer terribly before dying excruciating deaths. The problem is further compounded by these same cats reproducing before their death. Litters grow up, and despite the awful conditions, feral cat populations grow regardless of their agony. It is reasonable to assume that those who are run over–or are shot–are the lucky ones.

It is incomprehensible to me that governmental agencies that pass State and Federal laws to protect migratory birds do so little to protect them against such an effective enemy. There are cat populations right within the city that live on shorebirds (and handouts) which could be eliminated in what could be viewed as a win-win situation for all concerned. This do-nothing attitude we seem to have adopted allows the problem to grow, and wild animal populations to diminish.

In the water, we have marine mammals that can be found, and are studied by various people at Texas A&M University at Galveston. The most abundant of these is the **Bottle-nosed Dolphin**, common both in the gulf and the Atlantic. They are frequently seen off both ends of the island, as well as off the beach front. They pose no danger to humans, but their famous dorsal fin has provided a temporary shock to more than a few wade fishermen, including myself.

These highly intelligent creatures feed on schooling fish such

Dolphins Jumping

as mullet and seem to play most of the day in the surf. Being mammals, they must surface for oxygen, have tremendous endurance, and suckle their young that are born in our area. There are different identifiable pods at various locations around the island that forage in close proximity to humans.

All marine mammals, as well as sea turtles, are afforded complete protection by the government. It is strictly illegal to even possess a tiny portion of a dead one, and these laws are often enforced very strictly. If you find a dead or stranded dolphin on the beach, call the marine mammal stranding network at (409) 744-4455.

CHAPTER 7: **Land Birds Around the Island**

The birdlife on barrier islands is famous for radical changes as the year's seasons roll past. On Galveston Island, this is especially true. In winter, there are some insectivorous birds, but more excellent seed-eating birds hide within the fields and grasslands. Many birds of prey visit the island in winter to pick off the rats and mice that inhabit those same grasslands. The spring (and to a certain extent, fall) migration is famous for dozens of species of beautiful land birds, but they represent the briefest of avian guests in a rush to move elsewhere. And in summer, the land bird population reaches its low point of the calendar, with mostly the hale permanent residents hanging on in this hot, dry scrubland.

The major thrust of this chapter is to acquaint you with the more common land birds found here either in winter, summer, or both. Chapter 9 deals with the migrant birds separately, and Chapter 8, of course, covers the familiar waterbirds. Land birds are covered by groups, with some information on the more common species.

Winter birding for land varieties may be conducted in a number of areas, though species density is low. In town, there are the same ol' semi-domestic species found anytime of the year. A few possible birds of interest in town include the recently arrived Eurasian Collared Doves, present in the 25th St. neighborhood most commonly, occasional Bronzed Cowbirds back on Harborside Drive on wires, White-winged and Inca Doves all over town, and occasional warblers staying into early winter in some of the green spaces in town.

Sparrows are a great target on the island, with its fields and State Park readily accessible. After getting used to the barrage of Savannah Sparrows, one may find up to a dozen varieties in the different habitats available. Nelson's Sharp-tailed and Seaside Sparrows are present, but the crown jewel of the island's sparrows is the Le Conte's, which is actually fairly common in grasslands such as the State Park.

Raptors are also plentiful in winter. Red-tailed Hawks, Northern Harriers and American Kestrels are everywhere as winter residents, with a smattering of the year-round White-tailed Kites seen hovering or sitting on scrubby trees and wires. Other species are found less commonly or in the migration, but one cannot drive very far without seeing some avian hunter off in the distance.

Either in or not far from the few remaining woodlands forage the island's bug-eaters, such as kinglets, wrens, phoebes, two or three warblers and the occasional surprise. The Preserve may be the best place on the island to view some of these, with those insectivorous species found in the open areas not far away on the walkway.

Summer birding, especially looking for land birds, is about as exciting as the reruns of Ranger Walker. A few land birds like cardinals and mockingbirds are singing and nesting, but the vast majority of forest birds that breed at this latitude pass inland and shun what's left of our woods. However, the splendid Painted Bunting does nest in patches of forest remnants, and I must admit a certain pride at having this magnificent species raising its chicks right in my yard.

So here are the groups of land birds–excluding most migrants–that may be found in Galveston:

Birds of Prey

White-tailed Kite–This beautiful raptor is found in various forms all over the world, and its range has spread to many new locations over the past two decades. However, they have been on Galveston Island since "God and dirt," and since they tol-

Henslow's Sparrow, a rare visitor

erate mild deforestation, they seem to be in good shape at present. These rat-eaters may be identified by their black shoulder patch that earned them their former name of "Black-shouldered Kite," and, of course, a white tail. They frequently may be seen hovering, or perched near FM 3005. Up close, their red eyes add to their exquisite beauty, and allow them to hunt in low light conditions.

Northern Harrier—Harriers also eat rats, but rather than hunting from a perch, they fly over the marshes and grasslands on tilted wings, quickly diving down on hapless rodents. Males are gray and females brown, but the best field mark is the white rump patch at the base of the tail. In most of the South, this species is a winter resident, but it stays well into the summer at the State Park and may very well breed there.

Red-tailed Hawk—This handsome buteo rules over the open areas of the island, eating rabbits, rats, snakes and even feral cats. Great birds. They are brownish above and light below, and their reddish tail is diagnostic. Immatures lack the red tail, but their bulky bodies and lack of other buteo species here in winter easily identify them. Red-tails arrive in October and stay into early spring before departing westward.

Three other buteos: **Red-shouldered** and **Broad-winged Hawks** are found in the migration. They are told from red-tails by the heavily banded tails and smaller, slimmer bodies. See pictures, and also the uncommon **Swainson's Hawk.**

American Kestrel— Our smallest falcon, the kestrel is quite common along the wires going out FM 3005. Their diet of insects like grasshoppers turns to mice and small birds in October when they arrive here for the winter. They appear to be a reddish bird with a light underside, and the male is told by its bluish wings.

Other Falcons —Two other falcons may be seen occasionally around the island from fall through spring. The **Merlin** is scarcely larger than the slimmer kestrel but is dark and heavily streaked. The hefty **Peregrine**, common only in early October, is partial to artificial structures, and may be amazingly tame. Note the bold face patterns on all three falcons, and the long, pointed wings.

Osprey–This large hawk is a confirmed fish-eater, splashing down on top of its piscine quarry with talons outstretched. Not closely related to other birds of prey, it occupies a family of its own. They superficially resemble an adult Bald Eagle (seldom found here), but have a black mask through the eye and a white belly. Few spend the summer in our area.

Bald Eagle– Our National Bird is very rare on Galveston Island. I have seen one only as close as Freeport, and am frankly suspect of sightings by novices (since the experts almost never see them). Ospreys and Caracaras are most often confused, but I have even seen neophytes call Red-tailed Hawks Bald Eagles. Moreover, many Bald Eagles are the dark immatures which bear no resemblance to most peoples' image of the species.

Crested Caracara– The National Bird of Mexico, this hawk is actually closely related to falcons but occupies the same general niche as vultures. It also resembles Bald Eagles, but has a red bill, black tail band, and white wing-tips. This species seems to be increasing on Galveston, and has a small resident population often seen along Stewart Road. It is sometimes called "Mexican Eagle."

Some raptors are not regularly found on Galveston Island, such as Black Vulture, Mississippi and Swallow-tailed Kites, White-tailed Hawk and Bald Eagle. Of those that are, their status is:

Turkey Vulture	Uncommon winter resident October through April
White-tailed Kite	Common permanent resident and breeder
Sharp-shinned Hawk	Found in winter and spring, but numerous in fall
Cooper's Hawk	Common in the migration
Red-tailed Hawk	Common winter resident, October through early spring

Red-shouldered Hawk	Uncommon migrant, more of a fall bird
Broad-winged Hawk	Uncommon, only in migration
Northern Harrier	Common September through May; may breed in State Park!
Osprey	Regular winter resident; rare in summer
Crested Caracara	Irregular year-round; may be increasing
Peregrine	Rare winter resident; most common late September and early October
Merlin	Uncommon winter resident; found in migration, especially fall
American Kestrel	Common winter resident

Owls:

Barn Owl- This is a remarkably common bird west of the city. Its white underparts and monkey face are diagnostic. Brownish back is beautiful, and appetite for rats is even better! These are often seen around dusk flapping laboriously over fields. Very common in Indian Beach.

Great Horned Owl- This huge bird is an uncommon resident on the island. They eat large mammals, and may be told from Barn Owls by the dark underside. Song is eight soft hoots.

Other owls such as the Short-eared are found only on very rare occasions.

Non-Passerine Land Birds Familiar to Galveston

Quail- The Northern Bobwhite is probably extirpated from the island.

Doves- Five species of doves inhabit the island, mostly staying within the city limits. They can be identified as doves by their fast flight and pointed wings.

66

Mourning Dove- Slender, grayish brown bird with no outstanding marks. Long, pointed tail is diagnostic. Hunted widely on the island, and much more common from fall through spring.

Inca Dove- Smaller than the Mourning, with reddish patches in the wing and a scaly pattern on the back. Long tail with white outer tail corners make ID easy. Usually along sidewalks and yards.

Rock Dove- Highly variable "city pigeon" found all over the island. Now considered a wild bird.

Ground Dove- Uncommon and possibly disappearing, the Ground Dove has a short tail, but the reddish wings of an Inca Dove. Usually seen in late fall away from the city.

Eurasian Collared Dove- A recent immigrant, this bird is increasing downtown and into much of East Texas. Large dove with a long, banded, squared-off tail and inconspicuous black collar.

Woodpeckers are not common birds on the island. The **Red-bellied Woodpecker** is the most frequently seen resident, and is easily recognized by its ladder back and red cap. A few tiny **Downy Woodpeckers** reside in wooded areas, though scarce. The **Yellow-bellied Sapsucker** arrives for winter and is common though retiring in oaks and other tree species. The **Northern Flicker** is a late fall migrant, but normally absent from the island.

Familiar Songbirds

Absent of the migration, songbirds are not as plentiful as many places, but a healthy population of certain species are found on the island, either as summer or winter residents, or all year. The following is a synopsis of the more common, *non-migrant* songbirds. Birds only found in spring and/or fall are discussed in Chapter 9.

Eastern Phoebe- This our only wintering flycatcher. It has a large, dark head, and a peculiar habit of bobbing its tail repeatedly. They are normally seen near the island's water sources and are common from October through March. Listen for their loud chip and *Fe-oh-bee* song. Also found near water, though rare on the island, the gaudy **Vermillion Flycatcher** seems almost too red to be true. Strong late fall cold fronts may deliver this species to our area.

Horned Lark- This handsome bird of the grasslands is a year-round resident of both ends of the island. Note the yellow front with a black bib. These beach lovers have high-pitched call note much like a pipit.

Blue Jay- This species is regular on the island in small numbers. Their cousins the crows are absent–a product of the family's fear of crossing water. Found in neighborhoods and forests.

Brown Creeper- An exquisite visitor on late fall cold fronts, found mostly in forests with oaks.

<u>Nuthatches:</u> **Brown-headed** (now gone) formerly breeding; **Red-breasted** is occasional in late fall.

Carolina Chickadees and Tufted Titmice are not on the island, but are common elsewhere.

<u>Wrens</u> of four species are common on the island, especially in winter. The **Carolina** is a non-migratory, familiar wren of the woods, whose loud song is often heard. The **House Wren** is a winter resident, extremely common in scrubby areas. **Sedge Wrens** are also winter visitors, but are in tall grassy acreage. **Marsh Wrens** may be found year round in, well, marshes. :)

<u>Mimic Thrushes</u> are represented abundantly by the **Northern Mockingbird,** whose population is augmented in the winter. Also in the cooler months, **Brown Thrashers** appear where trees and brush are found. **Gray Catbirds** are common spring/fall migrants, rare in winter.

American Robin-Unmistakable and noisy. Some years found on late fall cold fronts; other years they stay all winter, and some years absent. Eats primarily berries in cool months.

Loggerhead Shrike-This hawk in a songbird's body lives mostly west of town, most often seen on wires hunting grasshoppers, small birds, mice, lizards and ribbon snakes. Note a large head, black mask, thick bill, gray back and white underside. Impales food on thorns and barbed wire.

American Pipit-This brownish-gray species is found in fields or near water, and walks moving its head like a pigeon. Flushes with burst of high chips (sometimes heard overhead) somewhat like Horned Lark's calls, and white outer tail feathers. See also rare **Sprague's Pipit.**

Ruby-crowned Kinglet is a very common, chatty bird with great nervousness and extremely tiny size. They are dull greenish with wing-bars and eye-ring. A winter resident, they sometimes display their "crown," like their rare cousin, the **Golden-crowned,** which is only present some years. Both mix with other wintering songbirds, and are quite vocal.

Blue-gray Gnatcatcher-A light-gray bird with a thin bill and high-pitched notes like Alvin the Chipmunk. Early spring migrant, coinciding with sand gnat outbreaks. Note cocked, long tail.

Cedar Waxwing-Sporadic winter visitor, often in good numbers. Loves mulberries. Leaves in early spring, then more southern-wintering birds arrive headed north late spring. Thin, high calls betray their presence.

"Black" Birds-Grackles are the most common of the black songbirds. **Great-tailed Grackles** are abundant residents all over the island, with their raucous calls and huge roosts downtown. A smaller species, the **Common Grackle,** is more slender and both sexes are blackish (other two have brown females). The **Boat-tailed Grackle** is less common, mostly found around marshes. They differ from Great-tails by having dark eyes, different calls and a rounded top of the head.

Red-winged Blackbird males are unmistakable with their crimson shoulders, and females are unique with their brown, heavy streaks. Red-wings may be seen any season. A bird their size that lacks any color but iridescence is the **Brewer's Blackbird,** a winter visitor. **Brown-headed Cowbirds** are seen spring through fall. **Bronzed Cowbirds** are scarce, except in late spring, but are occasionally found on Harborside Drive. **European Starlings** have short tails and stubby bodies, and will wander from the city to pastures. They are not closely related to true Blackbirds.

Eastern Meadowlark-A common grassland bird west of the city, sitting atop bushes and posts. Note brown back, white outer tail feathers, yellow front and black bib–all characters of birds that live in this habitat (see pipits and Dickcissel). Loud chatter and clear whistling song distinctive.

American Goldfinch-This lovely finch winters in small numbers on the island, though in their drab winter coat. They quickly come to feeders with seeds, but depart the island by early March. Occasionally mixing with goldfinches is the **Pine Siskin,** which I've recorded once on the island.

House Sparrow-This European transplant is not a true sparrow. Common in the cities and seen at times in farmland to the west. Boldly colored male; note cap and eye-stripe of female.

<u>True Sparrows</u>-How dedicated a birder are you? The ubiquitous **Savannah Sparrow** joins all other true sparrows as winter residents, but is just about everywhere. **Nelson's Sharptailed** and **Seaside Sparrows** may be found in the salt marshes with a little muddy walking. The highly prized **Le Conte's** is found easily in tall grass prairie (though good looks are hard) by sorting through the Savannahs. **Swamp** and **Lincoln's** are in the wetter areas, while **Chipping** are in loose flocks in late fall and sometimes spring. **White-throateds** are regular in late fall and sometimes winter, and **Song Sparrows** are fairly common in hedges and the shores of marshes. Less

Boat-Tailed Grackle (female)

common are the **White-crowneds, Grasshoppers, Clay-coloreds** and **Lark Sparrows** of the migration.

Although many of our land bird species are adapted for fields and other open areas, it is terribly important that we save what trees (and brush) we have. These are needed for feeding areas, and provide homes in which to nest. And this says nothing about the migrating birds in spring and fall. Birds. Trees. The two go together like deforestation and extinction.

Grasshopper Sparrow

Chapter **8: Waterbirds of Galveston**

Truthfully, there are many places on the Texas coast, and some parts east of our great state, that are excellent for land birds. High Island, a few miles to the east of Galveston, may be the most famous hammock in the New World for spring migrants (although our Laffite's Cove Nature Preserve is *mighty* good!). But Galveston has something added that is hard to beat: water birds.

There is simply no place like Galveston, when it comes to the combination of water birds *and* land birds. Both ends of the island are great for shorebirds such as plovers and sandpipers, and the numbers and diversity of gulls and terns can be staggering. And when you get your fill of marine birds at the island's ends, try a trip down Stewart Road to see the wealth of freshwater birds in the ponds, marshes and bays just west of the city.

There are other water bird viewing opportunities that are easy to miss. For those who love loons, Offat's Bayou along 61st Street offers good looks at these primitive divers from October through May, with the occasional Pacific or Red-throated Loon joining the abundant Commons. There are large, rectangular ponds all over the island where dirt was borrowed to build up the land for residences and businesses. These are excellent for ducks, shorebirds and other aquatic creatures. And if pelagic birds are your bag, the 25th St. (Flagship) Pier has free parking well out over the water. A leisurely period in your car, perhaps eating fast food for lunch, might yield gannets or jaegers, plus a plethora of sea birds just passing by. The fishing's not bad, either!

The migration is excellent for many species of sandpipers, and Galveston has the added luxury of pastures and golf courses

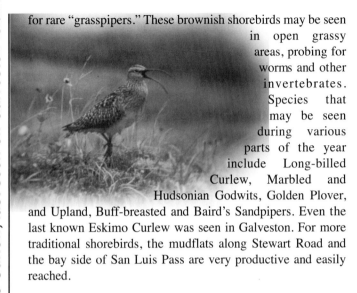

for rare "grasspipers." These brownish shorebirds may be seen in open grassy areas, probing for worms and other invertebrates. Species that may be seen during various parts of the year include Long-billed Curlew, Marbled and Hudsonian Godwits, Golden Plover, and Upland, Buff-breasted and Baird's Sandpipers. Even the last known Eskimo Curlew was seen in Galveston. For more traditional shorebirds, the mudflats along Stewart Road and the bay side of San Luis Pass are very productive and easily reached.

But with all the wonderful water bird migrants passing through in fall, and especially spring, and with all the multitudes of water birds that winter around Galveston, the usefulness of the island and its bay to birds might be greatest in summer. Each year, thousands of gulls, terns, waders and other water birds nest and raise their young in nearby Galveston Bay–including some whose populations are in serious jeopardy. Indeed, our fair island is a water bird wonderland, and makes Galveston, for my money, *THE* top birding location in North America.

So let's talk about what water birds are here, when they are found, and where. We have already mentioned loons, and **grebes** are common as well. Pied-billeds are residents in freshwater ponds, ditches and canals around the island, though their numbers are augmented in winter. But often hanging out with the loons are Eared Grebes, normally in the saltwater areas around the island. This species seems to frequently be found in small flocks within a few yards of shore in the gulf, especially after the passage of frontal systems. By May they leave and return in October.

Pelicans are a big favorite with local people, and Galveston has plenty of both species. Browns are most common along the gulf beach, diving into deeper water for their fishy lunch. Whites are winter residents, arriving in October with a few stragglers staying until late spring. This huge species usually is seen resting in large flocks (of course, *any* flock of White Pelicans is a *large* flock) on bars off either end of the island. They are separated ecologically from the Browns by their habitat because they feed in shallow water. They swim in formation, herding fish into shallower water and scooping them with their cavernous beaks.

Cormorants are equally well represented. The slender Neotropic Cormorant is a resident of the quieter bodies of water such as ponds, canals and lagoons. The bulky Double-crested tends to prefer more open bodies of water, and most leave for the North in spring. Telling these two apart is tricky, but look for the thicker bill and shorter tail in the Double-crested, and the white around the face in the Neotropic adults.

The **Magnificent Frigatebird** opens its eight-foot wingspan over Galveston from May through September, plucking jellyfish out of the water and robbing gulls of their meals. This great bird, abundant in the tropics, may be totally black (males), have a white chest (females), or have a white head as immatures. They are most often seen off the Bolivar Ferry, or in Christmas Bay.

Wading birds

Herons and egrets are among the most familiar of all water birds. Their long legs and neck make them easy to spot, and they often sit out in the open for a long look. Galveston supports virtually all North American herons, egrets and bitterns, plus ibis and spoonbills. They are best seen along Stewart Road, but are also fairly common on the ends of the island as well.

<u>Herons</u> are mostly dark waders with straight bills. The grand-fatherly **Great Blue Heron** is found in all seasons, and widespread on the island. Its tall stature and bluish-gray color makes it quite unmistakable, though the immatures are pretty plain. The **Little Blue Heron** is found sparingly in marshes, and is easily told from its larger cousin. **Tri-colored Herons** are common, especially in salt marshes, and may be separated from Little Blues by their white bellies. In early spring, **Green Herons** are found mostly in spring around the island's freshwater. Their orange legs, small size, loud call and diminutive size make them pretty hard to miss.

<u>Night Herons</u> are stocky, medium-sized birds seen skulking in vegetation by day, waiting for nightfall to emerge. **Black-crowns** tend to roost in salt cedars around freshwater ponds, but are not common winter birds. **Yellow-crowns** prefer to spend their days in salt marshes, though they become scarce in summer. Both breed on the mainland. Adults are easy to distinguish, but the young can be tough. My advice is to compare the length of the legs–those of Black-crowns being much shorter. Even at a great distance in the air, trailing legs of a night heron can be used to identify a Yellow-crowned, because in Black-crowns, the feet hardly extend past the tail.

<u>Egrets</u> are as abundant as herons, and easy to sort out as well. The huge **Great Egret** is quite unmistakable, but a quick check of its yellow bill and black legs will confirm your ID. The much smaller **Snowy** has a black bill and legs, with the famous yellow feet for scaring up fish off the bottom. In terrestrial areas such as pastures, **Cattle Egrets** appear, with their yellow feet and bill confirming an identification that can almost be made on ecology alone. Our birds are migrants, and are scarce in winter. In spring they add some brownish buff to the cap, back and chest.

The crown jewel of waders is the **Reddish Egret.** This stunningly beautiful, medium-sized bird is found in small numbers

75

along the Texas Coast, where the dark phased bird predominates. It is a dark bird with a reddish neck and two-toned bill. The white color phase (a permanent color) is found frequently in the San Luis Pass bay side, and is told by the two-toned bill (black in winter) and grayish-blue legs. Reddish Egrets are famous for running after their piscine prey or standing still with wings outstretched. This act lures unsuspecting fish into the shade, leading to their untimely death. They also use their wings to cut the glare on the water and see the fish better.

Two species of **ibis** are found on Galveston Island, with their names sounding much more alike than they look. The **White Ibis** is white with black wing-tips, and its legs range from dull orange in fall and winter to red in spring. Immature birds are brownish on top but are conspicuously white below. The **White-faced Ibis** is iridescent bronzy with greenish wings, though they often appear black at a distance. In spring, though, a narrow white facial line appears which goes *behind* the eye (as opposed to a very rare **Glossy Ibis**). Ibis are quite common in marshes and flooded fields.

The rare **Wood Stork** is occasionally seen on the mainland, and is to be looked for on the island.

The **Roseate Spoonbill** is a real crowd pleaser, well known and much loved among island folks. Their pink color occasionally earns them the "flamingo" misidentification, and this color comes from the shrimp they sift in wet areas (as it does in flamingos, which are not wild in Texas). The Roseates are most common in the warm months, and by no means a rare bird.

Sandhill Cranes are another big favorite with locals, as they are common in winter and easily recognizable. Their huge gray bodies and red caps may be seen standing around in pastures along FM 3005, and their raucous rattle may be heard for miles. Though built like a water bird, they are quite terrestrial in their ecology, eating plant material and a few small animals. They arrive in late October and begin disappearing by late February.

<u>Waterfowl</u>

<u>Ducks and Geese</u> may be extremely abundant on Galveston Island at various times of the year, and some species even breed here. In early fall, **Blue-winged Teal** arrive first, mostly on their way to more southerly wintering grounds in the tropics. By late fall, many species of ducks have arrived in the ponds and estuaries around the island. Late fall cold fronts also see the passing of large flocks of **Snow Geese** and more modest numbers of **White-fronted Geese**, flying northeast up the island, following the coastline.

Puddle ducks such as **Northern Shoveler**, **Green-winged Teal** and **Gadwall** accumulate in all the freshwater bodies, especially along Stewart Road. In spring, **American Wigeon** and returning Blue-winged Teal pile up in these same areas, staging for their flights up north to breed. The **Northern Pintail, Wood Duck** and **Mallard** are less common at these times, but may be found. Some ducks breed on the island. **Mottled Ducks**, resembling dark female Mallards, are common year round, and nest in many ponds and marshes on the island. Some **Fulvous Whistling-ducks** arrive in spring and nest in small numbers. And a scant number of **Blue-winged Teal** may nest on the island as well, before departing in late summer. Teal are also seen flying parallel to the coastline in spring headed northeast, a few hundred yards out–often in big numbers. Lastly, **Wood Ducks**, a resident of the dense

Ducks Jumping

swamps of the South, occasionally visit the island for a little sun and fun.

Diving ducks may be found fall through spring around Galveston. **Lesser Scaups** are seen most commonly around East Beach, occasionally in large flocks. The dark head and light back of the male, and the white facial circle of the female, make them easy to identify. Joining scaups are **Red-breasted Mergansers** (and, rarely, **Hooded Mergansers**), a curious fish-eating duck of shallow, saltwater lagoons and along the beachfront. Most appear to be females, but in late winter the gaudy males may be seen, often in large, sexually segregated flocks.

In some lakes on the island, the unique **Ruddy Duck** may be easily found, with its squatty body and stiff tail. Other diving ducks are rare, such as **Bufflehead**, **Canvasback, Redhead**, **Greater Scaup**, **Hooded Merganser**, **Common Goldeneye** and **Ring-necked Duck**. Occasionally, flocks of scoters are seen over the gulf during rainy late fall cold fronts flying northeast.

Rails

These odd birds may be found on Galveston, either skulking though marsh grass or out in the open swimming. The **Clapper Rail** is a permanent resident of the salt marshes, and widely sought by birders. They are most easily seen on Sportsman Road and in Apfell Park. The smaller, short-billed **Sora** spends the cooler months in a few marshes, but is uncommon and retiring. **Virginia Rails** are probably also present, but their secretive habits make them hard to find.

Some rails make no attempt to hide, and these may be seen on trips to the marshes. **American Coots** are common on the island from fall to spring, often forming large flocks in lakes and open areas in marshes. **Common Moorhen** may be found, especially in the cooler months, in the same habitat with coots. But in late spring, the splendid **Purple Gallinule** passes through Galveston, and may be seen in freshwater marshes along Stewart Road.

Shorebirds

The huge order Charadriiformes is found in incredible numbers from one end of the island to the other. Made up primarily of plovers, sandpipers, gulls and terns, fifty species or more may be considered regular at some time on the island. They inhabit areas from pastures to mudflats, and all along the shorelines. Some of our rarest birds are in this huge order.

Plovers usually are chunky birds with large eyes and big heads. They feed by picking up morsels off the sand or mud with their short bills, and some actually nest on the island. The Killdeer is a resident who says its name noisily, and nests in driveways and lawns. The two rings are all one needs to separate them from other plovers, which usually do not share their habitat.

Four species of ringed plovers occupy the beach. The tiny **Snowy** and **Piping Plovers** spend the winter months on each end of the island. While both have light backs, Snowies are separated by gray legs, while the latter has orangish legs (and a complete ring). The **Semipalmated Plover** is the same size with a dark back, and is also not uncommon in the same places. A larger plover that breeds on our beaches is the **Wilson's Plover**, and may be told by its thick, black bill.

By far our most common plover is the **Black-bellied**, who is found all around the island where a bare shoreline exists. Largely a winter resident, it is actually pure white underneath while here, and doesn't molt into its black belly until shortly before leaving for its Arctic nesting grounds. A close relative is the amazing **Golden Plover**, which migrates from the Arctic to southern South America and back! They may be seen on their northward trek in March and April, but seldom in the gaudy breeding plumage that gives them their name. These two species, which both have black bellies in breeding plumage, may be separated in winter plumage by the black under the wing of the Black-bellied, its thicker bill and the grayer body contrasting to the brown of the Golden.

Three species of remarkably beautiful shorebirds which are

neither plovers nor sandpipers are the **American Avocet**, **Black-necked Stilt,** and **American Oystercatcher**. Avocets are winter birds that are seen in large flocks in the migration. The white stripe on the wing at rest is quite diagnostic, as is the bizarre, upturned bill. In spring, their head and neck gets buffy, and they become even more beautiful. Their close relative the stilt is more common in warm months, but may be seen in Apfell Park in winter. These noisy birds nest in salt marshes around Galveston and are striking birds with their pink legs and bold black and white coloration.

Oystercatchers are uncommon but regular at both ends of the island. Their compressed, red bill and pink legs also stand out against the black and white body, with their red eyes giving the bird's appearance additional character. Their feeding style, unique among the birds, has them slipping their slender bill between the shells of clams and oysters, snipping the muscle, and eating the soft-bodied creature when the shell falls helplessly open.

<u>Sandpipers</u> are an extremely diverse and abundant group of birds. They're more slender than the plovers, but with longer bills to probe down into the sand and mud on which they feed. There are two exceedingly common sandpipers on the island, which are a must for every birder to quickly learn. The **Willet** is a large, noisy, gray bird of the beaches whose identity can be confirmed by the black and white stripes in the wings in flight. Most Willets depart in spring for the North, but a few stay and inhabit our salt marshes to raise their young in summer. Their gray coloration gives way to brown, and barring appears on their undersides.

Winter Avocets and a Laughing Gull

Lesser Yellowlegs heading down the coastline

The **Sanderling** is our most abundant shorebird, forever seen scurrying around on the beach and running off unwanted beachmates. It is hardly larger than a sparrow, with a black bill and legs and a whitish body. Though most leave in late spring for the Arctic, some of these busy little guys stay all year long. Their probing into the sand has often been likened to a sewing machine, and this behavior is not mimicked by other small sandpipers.

Aside from these two species, there are many types of sandpipers that may be found some or all of the year, generally excluding summer. One common pair is the **Greater and Lesser Yellowlegs**. Greaters are nearly the size of a Willet, and are essentially winter residents. Lessers are generally absent in winter, but are abundant in the migration. Fall sees flocks of 10-20 flying down the island SW to Mexico, and the same flocks returning in the opposite direction in spring. **Solitary Sandpipers** are closely related to Lesser Yellowlegs, and are seen at the same times. Watch for the eye ring, the spots on the back, and the dark legs in these loners.

Peeps are tiny sandpipers that are found in different places and times on the island. **Western Sandpipers**, with black legs and a thin bill that droops at the tip, are common winter residents on our beaches and tidal flats. **Least Sandpipers** are also winter birds but have yellowish legs and more brown coloration. They seem to like smaller bodies of water like ponds and ditches. The **Semipalmated Sandpiper** suddenly appears in

mid-spring, and again in early fall, and can be quite numerous. Their grayish bodies and thick, short bills separate them from the other two common peeps that hang around for the winter.

Three peeps, the **White-rumped, Baird's and Buff-breasted Sandpipers**, are late spring migrants and are seen again in early fall. The former is found along shores, while the latter two are more grasspipers. Those not experienced with the White-rumped need to flush this bird to confirm its ID, but the elongate body (like a Baird's) and fine streaking on the chest really help. Those looking for the Baird's need to watch for the scaly back pattern.

Dunlins and dowitchers may be abundant on the island from fall to spring and are well worth learning. Dunlins are sanderling-sized, with a longish bill that droops considerably on the end. They are very plain gray with a white underside, until they get ready to leave in spring. At this time, their black bellies and reddish backs make them unmistakable. Dowitchers are larger but also gray, with a white back that shows in flight. They have extremely long bills, and are divided into two species, the Short-billed and the Long-billed. The former prefers saltwater shorelines, while the latter opts for freshwater. They turn reddish in the spring also. Distinguishing the two is hazardous, so check a field guide!

Ruddy Turnstones are basically a plover in a sandpiper's body. They have developed the short bill, chunky body, neck ring and surface-feeding habits of plovers, but its sandpiper morphology may be seen in its skeleton and musculature. Turnstones flip over shells and rocks looking for tiny amphipods and other invertebrates, and, well, seem to leave no stone unturned.

Spotted Sandpipers are unique birds that hunt insects around rocks and pilings. They bob their rear ends up and down, and fly with stiff, almost paddle-like wings. All winter, they are dull gray with light underparts. But in spring, they get their spots, and really become a beautiful bird!

Godwits and curlews are big brown shorebirds that are more often seen in pastures than shores. The former has a slightly upturned, two-toned bill, while the latter has a strongly decurved beak.

Marbled Godwits are common winter residents, which may be seen on mudflats as much as the grasslands. The highly sought **Hudsonian Godwit** may be seen in spring on its way to Hudson Bay to breed. **Long-billed Curlews** are also winter residents, but their smaller cousin the **Whimbrel** is normally only seen in its spring migration.

A somewhat smaller brownish bird of the grasslands is the **Upland Sandpiper**. Appearing in mid-spring and early fall, it stands out in pastures with alert eyes and amazing camouflage. Smaller still, is the **Pectoral Sandpiper**, at home both in grassland, as well as muddy shores. The sharp demarcation between the dark chest and white belly is an excellent field mark. **Stilt Sandpipers** are common at about the same time, but seem to prefer lagoons and mudflats.

The last three sandpipers are somewhat unique for various reasons. The **Common Snipe** is found in wet, grassy fields as a winter resident and is a far cry from the mythological creatures we all hunted as kids. The long bill and excellent camouflage make it a very interesting bird, and its *kreek!* call will wake us up when one flushes.

The **Red Knot** is a chunky sandpiper found as an uncommon winter resident and migrant along the open beach, probing with its rather short bill.

A great story in biology is the **Wilson's Phalarope**, which appears late spring and returns in early fall. They breed up north, but winter at sea. The females are larger than males, more colorful, and are mated to several males. She rules the roost, and keeps the males feeding the hungry chicks. This species is found along shores when passing through and is not an uncommon bird.

There is a group of sea birds called **jaegers** that are uncommon in the Gulf of Mexico, but rarely are seen from shore.

However, jaegers are occasionally seen from the shores of Galveston in the cooler months, and possibly the best place is off the 25th Street (Flagship) pier. Pomarine is the more regular species seen, with a few records of Parasitic. If you see these falcon-like sea birds, try to compare their size to a nearby bird like a Laughing Gull and check the field guide.

Galveston may be the finest place on the gulf coast for **gulls,** with five regularly occurring types joined by visitors from both the Atlantic and Pacific systems. In one two-week span in late fall of 1997, I recorded 10 species at East Beach. That's an amazing diversity for any place! The following is a summary of our normally occurring gulls in Galveston.

Our largest gull is the **Herring Gull.** Adults are quite white with light gray mantles, much like the smaller **Ring-billed Gull.** But the obviously larger size and lack of bill ring easily identifies them to species. The immatures are brown all over, with the brownish underside separating them from immature Ring-billeds. These two larger species are winter residents, arriving in October and thinning out in April. A few non-breeders turn pale and spend the summer here.

Laughing Gulls are abundant residents on the island, being quite familiar to us human residents. In fall and winter they lack the black head, but it begins appearing in February. Spring calls for them to head to the small islands in Galveston Bay, where there're thousands of pairs of nesters. A very similar species to the Laughing Gull is the **Franklin's.** It passes through unobtrusively in late fall in winter plumage, and may be seen in small numbers in October and November. Check the field guide, but this bird tends to stand shorter in flocks than Laughing Gulls and, therefore, may be overlooked. In spring, it can be seen in low numbers in April in breeding plumage after the passage of frontal systems. Check the white in the wing-tips.

The **Bonaparte's Gull** is a tiny bird that feeds like a butterfly over the rough surf along Seawall and may be seen resting on both ends of the island. Watch for the unique wing pattern on adults and immatures, as well as the dark smudge on the side of the head in both plumages. This bird does not gain its black head until *after* it leaves in spring to nest up north.

<u>Terns</u> are amazingly abundant all over the island, with many species nesting in Galveston Bay. The **Forster's Tern** may be seen all year diving into the shallows not far from shore after small fish. Rather whitish birds, they blend in well with the beaches on which they rest and honestly seem to be everywhere. **Common Terns** are quite similar but are mostly spring/fall birds. Just watch for the light gray undersides of spring adult Commons and the dark horizontal bar on the wings of the juveniles (carpel bar). Forster's are very white and may have extremely long tails. This species feeds abundantly along the shores, but breeds in the salt marshes.

The tiny **Least Tern** appears suddenly in April with its *klee klee* notes, feeding in shallows for the tiny fish they feed their chicks. Also in spring comes the unmistakable **Black Tern,** which may be seen by the thousands at San Luis Pass in late spring and especially early fall. Adults are all dark, but even the young have dark backs, unlike any of our regular terns.

The less common **Gull-billed Tern** feeds in salt marshes along the island and may be identified by its short, blunt, black bill with the light gray back giving a clue often from long distances. The slightly larger **Sandwich Terns** appear in spring with the Gull-billed to nest in Galveston Bay and rests in big numbers along the beaches. Its black bill with a yellow tip

Royal Tern with Sandwich Terns

readily identifies it, and it may, at times, develop a pinkish hue on its chest. They feed deep with the Royals.

Our two largest terns are the size of gulls. The huge **Caspian**, the size of a Ring-billed Gull, patrols the shallows of our bays and estuaries for good-sized fish. Its thick, red bill is diagnostic, and dwarfs any Royals it sits next to on the beach. The **Royal Tern** feeds out deep, so it is a more slender bird. The beak is an orange-yellow and thinner than the massive bill on a Caspian. Royals breed by the thousands in the bay and in early fall become incredibly numerous.

The **Black Skimmer** is a real local favorite. Skimmers congregate by the hundreds on both ends of the island, and also breed in the bay. Their numbers suffered in the 1990's, and we hope the new millennium brings them good fortune. Skimmers are unique in that their lower mandible is the only one in the world longer than the upper one, made so to skim the water's surface for small fish. Their "bill snap reflex" allows them to flick fish into their gape without a thought, and the shallow lagoons around the island are perfect for these neat birds. Virtually the same color as a skimmer is the rare **Sooty Tern**,

Graceful Black Skimmers

seen occasionally after storms or strong southerly winds.

The last water bird is the **Belted Kingfisher.** They are common winter residents often seen on wires or hovering over water. Their long dagger bill and shaggy crest make them familiar and unmistakable. Females have a reddish band on the chest which is absent in the male.

That's a tremendous diversity and disparity of birds, especially for neophytes. However, we should be proud of what we have and try to set aside some of our wetlands for future generations to see these splendid birds.

On fish watch is the Belted Kingfisher

CHAPTER **9:**
That Fantastic Bird Migration

Galveston Island is a marvelous place for winter birding, with clouds of seabirds on both ends, ducks and waders strewn all along Stewart Road, and rarities such as Le Conte's Sparrow in tall grass fields. Summers are interesting, too, as many species of gulls, terns and waders nest in colonies on small islands adjacent to Galveston. But make no mistake about it, the spring bird migration on the Upper Texas Coast is unparalleled anywhere, anytime.

Beginning in March, climaxing in late April, and extending well into May with some of the top species to be seen, the spring bird migration in our area is as famous as it is astounding. Calm early mornings give way to frantic periods in the middle of the day, with literally dozens of song bird species dropping in all over the island. Warblers lead the charge, but flycatchers, vireos, tanagers, grosbeaks, buntings and orioles all join the migratory mosaic that decorates our trees with reds, greens, blues and other bright hues of avian color.

Other land bird families join the fray such as cuckoos and hummingbirds, and waterbirds are certainly well represented from the "grasspipers" in the fields to the myriads of other shorebirds along the coastline. On April 18, 1998, participants of the Upper Texas Coast Birding Festival were treated to 153 species just on Galveston Island. That is simply a staggering number of birds for an area which, by its nature, lacks crows and jays, tits, many woodpeckers and other birds.

That day was fantastic because it was a cold front day with rain and north winds causing the huge landfall that resulted in such great diversity. The first lesson to learn about spring bird migration is that inclement weather is our friend. Sunny days with gentle south winds are lovely to be outdoors in, but far less productive. However, even these days are excellent in the spring bird migration on the island, because some birds do make landfall, regardless of the weather.

The spring bird migration actually begins in late January when the first Purple Martin is sighted. Throughout most of February, martins are about the only non-wintering bird seen. March is a time to see many species of birds that breed in the South, like Great-crested Flycatchers, Ruby-throated Hummingbirds, Northern Parulas, waterthrushes, Red-eyed Vireos, and much more. They are familiar to us as summer breeders in the Deep South, and their appearance is a promise of the more northern breeders yet to come.

Sure enough, by April, more northern nesters such as Scarlet Tanagers, Baltimore Orioles, Rose-breasted Grosbeaks and a dizzying array of warblers descend on our modest canopies, providing a rich experience in ornithology unmatched in North America. Spilling well over into May, the parade continues with prized birds such as Mourning and Canada Warblers rushing through, and extralimital species such as Olive-sided and *Empidonax* Flycatchers are found into early June!

The fall migration here in the western Gulf is more modest but is unfortunately underestimated by birders. By late August, with the two rare warblers in the above paragraph reappearing, and all Eastern *Empidonax* Flycatchers easily found, many other species join in the great southbound journey. Orchard and Baltimore Orioles, almost blinding in their color, ease down the island southwest from canopy to canopy, and most Eastern warblers may be found through the end of September. This begins an odd time in fall though, as some days are mysteriously devoid of migrants, while other days produce excellent birding. Cold fronts, plenty welcomed by this time of year, bring birds through on their way south, but the timing of the wave of migrants is not always clear. But by late October, these northern blasts regularly bring wintering birds on their chilly winds. The fall season is capped off with large flocks of White-fronted and Snow Geese, Sandhill Cranes, and many species of ducks and shorebirds being transported to our area as the cool days of late fall descend upon us.

These fronts continue to move birds around virtually to the New Year, with White Ibis still on the move into January. But since January is the month our first martins are seen, it becomes clear that bird migration is practically a non-stop process throughout the year. Summer bears this out as some spring migrants show up in late June and even early July, while some fall migrants such as Least Flycatchers and Louisiana Waterthrushes appear in July on their fall plunge. Some martins, of course, are headed south in June, and even late May!

One of the reasons the spring bird migration is far more pop-ular than fall is that birds are very colorful during their north-ward trek, as they get ready for the nesting season. They're also about practicing their songs, so the air is full of trills and melodies. The mosquito population is a bit subdued in spring, compared to the droves that wander in fall, and this is helped by the relatively dry conditions that exist in spring along the coast. Plus, the weather itself is far more pleasant in spring than the first half of fall. This is due to the Gulf–still cool from the winter weather–making spring air refreshing, before the summer cranks up the heat and humidity. There is yet another reason spring is simply better birding:

Most birds migrate in a loop during the year. The majority of Eastern birds take an easterly route in fall, taking them along the Atlantic past Florida in their southward plunge. The west winds that precede fronts tend to "bend" their southward progress to the east. So with the exception of a few species mentioned earlier, most species simply migrate farther east than Texas in fall. Many we get are on the western edge of their migration range, or individuals resulting from an east wind following a frontal system. Sometimes prolonged east winds after fronts in October will bring us interesting species such as Black-throated Blue Warblers, and one period in 1996 delivered the extremely rare Connecticut Warbler into my lit-tle patch of forest.

But in spring, steered by the trade winds from the Caribbean, tens of thousands of birds descend on the Upper Texas Coast with a barrage of color, sound and diversity like nothing I've witnessed in forty years of birding. Slow days may produce a dozen species of warblers, and good days defy description. It's like the path to North America comes over the Gulf and through Galveston, so for a brief few weeks in mid-spring our lives are made richer by these beautiful visitors.

Of course, that's just the eastern birds. Sitting at our longitude, though, we get an inordinate number of western birds in both spring and fall. Treats like Black-headed Grosbeaks, Western Tanagers and Bullock's Orioles bring a Rocky Mountain flavor to the island, along with several species of warblers. Our close proximity to a more western habitat, as well as having vast open areas on the island, result in western birds such as caracaras frequently, and many others less commonly. This collection of western birds adds to the species richness of the island.

So where would one go to experience the spring bird migration? My advice would be to begin a morning of birding just west of the city on Stewart Road with the sun at your back. Check all the ponds for waterbirds and be sure to take 8-Mile Road out to Sportsman's Road for salt marsh birds. By the latter part of the morning, you are ready for the sanctuary called the Laffite's Cove Nature Preserve. Wearing unobtrusive colors with bug spray handy, and being as quiet as possible, slip into the Preserve and look for small birds in the trees. Upon finding a mixed flock, try to stay with them, making sure you record each species. The walk over the marsh and through the open area is great for a different set of birds, too. You will add dozens of woodland birds to the day just in this nature preserve. How fortunate we are that it was saved!

The State Park is worth a look, though trees are scarce. Then head out FM 3005 for the west tip, keeping a close eye on the pastures for grasspipers. These are brownish shorebirds of fields and other open areas, and often may produce some hard-to-find species. Look for Buff-breasted and Baird's

Sandpipers, curlews, godwits, and Golden Plovers. Plus, the last Eskimo Curlew ever seen was on our island, so dream the dream and watch for tiny curlews in early spring!

At the end of the island, you will find San Luis Pass to be replete with birds. Enter the beach on the south side and work slowly toward the bridge, looking over the shorebird flocks. A different species composition will be found on the bay side, with Whimbrels in spring, breeding Wilson's Plovers, Reddish Egrets (even white phased) and small sandpipers all found along the shoreline. Stay on the existing roads when you can, and be careful crossing soft, unforgiving sand.

By the time you've finished this area and have eaten lunch somewhere, it is time to return to the Preserve (with the sun at your back). It should have a new set of birds, and most of the migrants you saw earlier will have taken off for the mainland. Following this trek, you may drive the gauntlet down Seawall if you wish to bird more and head to Apfell Park on the east end. This entire area is great for birds in the migration, as well as winter, and many interesting species of shorebirds may be seen at very close range out your car window. The long lagoon along the east end of Seawall may have some good finds, too, as well as the marsh over the top of the ramp on the north side of Seawall. I've found phalaropes there on numerous occasions, as well as a great opportunity to scare the heck out of my passengers.

Some green spaces within the city may have migrants, such as Kempner Park. A good look at Offat's Bayou may reveal loons and grebes, with occasional rarities. Sitting on the end of the Flagship Pier (25th Street) has produced jaegers and gannets, as well as the odd sea ducks. Some people have even returned to the Preserve for a third visit late afternoon, and found new species having arrived tardily. If you have the time, the island has the birds!

The following is a breakdown of land birds with some of the more common species found in the migration on Galveston Island, as well as much of the Gulf Coast. Some species found elsewhere are absent as migrants from the island, and others are not found frequently enough to be included in this work. Comprehensive field guides will provide more details on what is possible but will include virtually everything in North America. Remember too, that many birds seen in the spring or fall may be common at other seasons and may be found in the land and water bird chapters. This is the status for (mostly) songbird families predominantly seen in the migration.

Non-Passerine Migrant Birds:

Ruby-throated Hummingbird –This tiny nectivore becomes amazingly common in early spring, and a few stay around the island in summer to breed. In September, their numbers pick up while they migrate south, and then they virtually disappear by the end of October. This species seldom winters in the area, but other species such as the Rufous visit in small numbers.

Chimney Swift– This dark, extremely fast insectivore zips across the Gulf in spring, and some spend the summer on the island. They look like cigars on long, slender wings, and fly fast with short wing strokes. Their high-pitched twittering is easily recognizable, especially in chimneys!

Yellow-billed Cuckoo– This odd bird is found in the spring migration, and a few will nest in Galveston. Note the brown back, clear underside and reddish in the wings. This "rain crow" often nests near caterpillars and makes its descending yuk-yuk-yuk note with increasing rapidity. The extremely secretive **Black-Billed** slips through in small numbers with the Yellow-billeds.

Common Nighthawk– This long-winged, erratic flier arrives in April and breeds on sandy or gravely patches of ground. Note the white bar on the wing and the nasal *kent* call. Scarce in fall. Watch for the western Lesser Nighthawk in late spring. Check the white wing bar position.

Chuck-will's Widow– A deep-brown bird that passes through the island in spring. Mistaken for Whip-poor-wills (rare on the island), they may be most easily found in the Preserve in April.

Songbirds (Passeriformes)

<u>Flycatchers</u> are most abundant late spring and early fall, with few winter or summer birds.

Eastern Kingbird	Very common April and May; less so in September
Western Kingbird	Uncommon April and May; rare in fall
Scissor-tailed Flycatcher	Very common in migration; rare in summer
Great-crested Flycatcher	Common April and May; uncommon in fall
Eastern Phoebe	Common winter resident October through April (see Chapter 7)
Olive-sided Flycatcher	Late spring and early fall; rare
Eastern Wood-Pewee	Common migrant (canopy edges; long aerial swoops)
Empidonax Flycatchers	May and early fall; (see field guide)

<u>Swallows</u> are seen in absolute multitudes sailing up and down the island in both migrations. In spring, many come in off the Gulf, but most fly along the coast, arriving from the Freeport area. In early fall, they begin an equally sizable exodus from North America, heading southwest back towards the Freeport region and along the coast to Mexico and parts beyond. Their swift flight on deep wingbeats identifies them as swallows, but assigning a species can be tough under some conditions. Try to see the chest, back color, and shape of the tail (for Barn Swallows).

Barn Swallows are our most common and easily recognizable swallow. Their reddish underparts and long, forked tail make their ID the easiest of the swallows. **Cliff Swallows**, which nest at San Luis Pass, have shorter tails but show no red underside. **Tree Swallows** are immaculate white underneath with greenish backs, while **Rough-winged** and **Bank Swallows** are brown on the back. The former has a dusky throat and chest (like a small, female martin) and the latter has a bold band across the chest.

Purple Martins, our largest swallows, are famous for their early arrivals, usually appearing in early February. Residents lure them with martin houses, and may see reduced insect populations for their trouble. Boxes should be wooden; and away from limbs, fairly high, and relatively clean.

<u>Thrushes</u> are great singers and well represented in Galveston, especially in spring. **American Robins** may be quite common some years and absent others. The unobtrusive **Hermit Thrush** is found in forests such as the Preserve from October into May. **Eastern Bluebirds** occasionally appear after fall cold fronts but will neither winter nor stay to nest.

A great challenge is the four transit thrushes, all looking very much like the **Hermit,** that migrate through the island in spring. **Wood Thrushes** have bold spots underneath and reddish heads. The **Veery** has a cinnamon back and few spots. The faces separate **Swainson's** and **Gray-cheeked Thrushes**; the former having a buffy eye ring and the latter a grayish face. Check field guide.

The following is a list of many more migrants found passing through Galveston. While there is no species description, pictures are available, and field guides will provide more help. Remember that the day's weather plays a big role in species composition and numbers!

<u>Vireos:</u>

White-eyed Vireo	Common early spring migrant; uncommon in fall
Red-eyed Vireo	Abundant spring migrant; less common in fall
Yellow-throated Vireo	Common spring migrant; uncommon in fall
Blue-headed Vireo	Common winter resident in woodlands

Philadelphia Vireo	Regular late spring migrant; rare in fall
Warbling Vireo	Regular in April and early May; rare in fall

Warblers:

Yellow-rumped	Abundant winter visitor; October through April
Orange-crowned	Common winter visitor; October through April
Palm	Uncommon winter resident
Blue-winged	Common in April; uncommon in fall
Golden-winged	Scarce in late spring; rare in fall
Tennessee	Common in spring and fall
Nashville	Uncommon in spring; more common in October
Yellow	Regular in late spring and fall
Chestnut-sided	Common late April and early May; early October
Magnolia	Common late April and early May; October
Cape May	Scarce in late spring; very rare in fall; SE winds
Black-throated Blue	Scarce in migration; east winds
Black-throated Green	Common in April and May; October
Blackburnian	Uncommon late spring and fall
Yellow-throated	Regular early spring; scarce in fall
Pine	Uncommon on late fall cold fronts
Prairie	Scarce in spring and early fall
Bay-breasted	Regular late April and early May, scarce in fall
Blackpoll	Regular late April and early May; rare in fall
Cerulean	Scarce in spring; very rare in fall
Black and White	Common in spring and fall
Prothonotary	Common in early spring;

	uncommon in early fall
Worm-eating	Common in early spring; uncommon in mid-fall
Swainson's	Regular in early spring; rare in fall; very secretive
Kentucky	Regular in April and September
Mourning	Uncommon in early May and early fall
Hooded	Common in early spring and regular in early fall
Wilson's	Regular spring and fall migrant
Canada	Uncommon in late spring and early fall

Warblers with other Names

Northern Parula	Common in early spring; less so in fall
American Redstart	Common in spring; regular in fall
Ovenbird	Common in spring; uncommon in fall
Northern Waterthrush	Common all spring; regular all fall
Louisiana Waterthrush	Regular in early spring uncommon in early fall;
Common Yellowthroat	Permanent resident, though scarce in summer
Yellow-breasted Chat	Regular spring and fall migrant; very secretive

<u>Miscellaneous Migrants:</u>

Baltimore Oriole	Common mid and late spring and early fall
Orchard Oriole	Common early spring and very early fall

Summer Tanager	Common all spring; scarce in fall
Scarlet Tanager	Common mid and late spring; scarce in fall
Rose-breasted Grosbeak	Common in mid-spring; uncommon in fall
Blue Grosbeak	Common spring; fairly common in fall
Indigo Bunting	Abundant in spring; common in October
Painted Bunting	Common in mid-April; scarce in fall; local breeder
Bobolink	Uncommon in late spring; rare in fall
Dickcissel	Very common late spring; common in fall; breeds in Indian Beach

Some may wonder why the bird migration is so excellent in Galveston. Part of it lies with the availability of habitats. In the water bird chapter, we discussed how the island has beach-front, mud flats, freshwater ponds and fresh and salt marshes, Offat's Bayou, and oceanic birds. The abundance of freshwater ponds is largely due to efforts to build up land in certain places with "borrowed" dirt. These "borrow pits" fill up with water and provide excellent habitat for ducks and other pond birds. Terrestrial habitats include many fruiting trees, deep forests like Laffite's Cove Nature Preserve, wooded neighborhoods in Galveston, open pastures for grasspipers, and fields full of sparrows and other grassland birds. All these habitats together make our fair island an attractive place to just about any migrating birds.

That only tells part of the story, though. There is a geographical reason that many people overlook. Our home is right on the edge of the curve where the Gulf Coast stops running east/west and will eventually run north/south, like around Corpus Christi. Being on the edge of this curve is a very advantageous location.

Many birds like *Empidonax* flycatchers, swallows and orioles prefer to fly around the Gulf of Mexico in early fall, so to take the shortest route, they head for the Galveston area, take a tight turn southwest, and head south down the Central Texas Coast. Many of these birds could miss most of the entire gulf coast, but contact it from here down to about Matagorda. Believe me, in early fall we get loads of these birds, stopping in for water and groceries.

In spring, the same sort of thing happens in reverse. Many birds avoid the wide expanse of the gulf and follow the Mexican shoreline north and continue up the Texas coast. When they arrive at the "bend," they probably spend their last days on the coastline right around Galveston before heading inland into the vast expanse of forests. Wonderful warblers like Mourning, Canada and Nashville fall into this category, and really make our area superior to those east of here. They are found east of here sometimes in spring and fall, but not in the numbers they are here.

The reason we have better birding in the migration than areas down the coast, like the Central and Lower Texas Coast is that we get many trans-Gulf migrants as well, and they get many fewer because their coastline runs parallel to the flight of these birds. So clearly, we get the best of both worlds: Trans-gulf *and* circum-gulf migrants.

Well, let's say you're really pumped up now about seeing some migrants and want to know how to maximize your bird experience here in this avian paradise. Let me make several suggestions about a day in the field, and you can plan a successful day from there:

1) **The season.** The peak of the spring bird migration is mid-April to early May, and the fall is from late August to early October. In spring especially, you may want to get out early and get used to the places, your binoculars, and some of the resident birds. No need to do this in fall, but be prepared for intense heat, humidity, bugs and cottonmouths if you do. Still, some of our neatest species, including some great sea birds, may be seen in August.

2) **The day.** If possible, try to pick birding days where there are cold fronts, or other inclement weather in spring. When birds are coming in off the water, they will drop down along the coast if the weather is threatening, or the wind is out of the north. In the fall, cold fronts bring birds with them, and birds suddenly appear as soon as bad weather hits in spring. All day rain in the migration is a rare event, so breaks between showers may be excellent for migrants.

3) **The route.** One issue to consider is the sun. In early morning, you may wish to work Stewart Road from the city out to the Preserve. The sun will be behind you and viewing is much easier then. You want to hit the Preserve late morning, as often there is a landfall of migrants at that time. But in fall, start your day at the Preserve, as many migrants may sleep there, feed for an hour or so, and depart.

Another matter to address is the tide. It really helps to be where there are shorebirds when there is a high tide. Otherwise, they could be feeding way out and sometimes beyond our sight. Do not approach shorebirds straight-on, but rather drive or walk parallel to shore. They need their rest, and getting a close look without flushing them is sometimes important. A word of caution, though: beware of "Beaumont mud." You can ride along the beach with a hard bottom for miles, and all of a sudden sink to your ears–where no truck can get out and no truck can *pull* you out. By all means, hose off your vehicle after being on the beach, or go through a car wash. Incidentally, shorebirds are often approached closer by car than on foot.

If you bird the entire day and the whole island, it becomes necessary to drive through Galveston at some point. My suggestion is to save the east end for afternoon. This way, you are facing east with the sun at your back. Some people like to be at East Beach near sundown, especially in late fall and winter, as gulls and some other water birds arrive late to roost. The beach is pretty hard here, but do not even *think* about going past the barricade onto the Apfell Park beach. If the cops and Beaumont mud don't get you, I will. There are nesting shorebirds along this stretch, and the public has actually accepted this minor restriction.

Given the preceding paragraph, the best strategy probably is to head "through town" sometime well after lunch. But to see more birds, take 61st Street to check Offat's Bayou for loons, grebes and whatever, and continue on 61st until it dead ends a half-mile later on a bumpy old road. This area has fruiting trees, and in the migration, it can be very productive. Then, get on Broadway (the extension of I-45 through town) and take the 51st Street exit over to Pelican Island. From the bridge and causeway you may see interesting sea birds like flocks of Eared Grebes, pelicans, and waders. The last dirt road on the left is a perfectly horrid road but dead ends at a wonderful marsh and lagoon. If you suffer through the bumps and pot-holes (you won't get stuck) you will find an array of water-birds any season and excellent migrants at the beginning of the ordeal. Painted Buntings nest here in summer, and chats are found in the migration. If migrants are present, you might walk further on the paved road, looking over the mulberries to your left.

When you finish with Pelican Island, go back to Broadway and hang a left. It takes you through town much faster than Seawall, which you will eventually connect with east of town. Take the Seawall east to Apfell Park and turn right just before Seawall ends. This area is good for Clapper Rails, shorebirds, waders and waterfowl. Then continue out onto East Beach and angle over to the left toward the jetties. Birders may wish to buy an annual VIP pass for ten bucks, and come as often as you like. This may be the top location in the country for rare gulls. When you are out of light and have no choice but to quit birding, return on Seawall and choose one of Galveston's fine seafood restaurants, and you will then agree that few places on earth can compare with the birdlife on this magical island – or the fresh seafood.

CHAPTER 10: The Future of Galveston Island

The island on which we live is an incredibly fragile ecosystem. It is subject to torrential rains, searing heat, annual prolonged drought, roaring winds, and sudden variations in salinity–to name a handful of natural stress elements. But this is the nature of barrier islands, and the inhabitants that belong here have learned to cope over the millennia. Birds and some other animals migrate to escape harsh conditions, reptiles and amphibians aestivate during drought and hibernate while cold grips the island, arthropods die leaving their eggs in the soil while unfavorable conditions exist; other invertebrates like fiddler crabs ride out lean times in their burrows, and mammals somehow find a way to survive just about anything.

Anyone who wants to study natural selection–how the hardy overcome adversity–need go no further than our fair island. The wildlife of Galveston has had the full gamut thrown at them and has responded with thousands of years of natural selection and refinement. Gnatcatchers know just when to come through for gnats, kingsnakes have an uncanny way of knowing when the last cold spell is over, and certain amphibians have learned to wait for the August rains to end the long drought and provide the much needed ephemeral ponds for reproduction.

I am reminded of the people of Galveston. Survivors. Storm after storm, literally and figuratively, we have overcome the winds of time like few places on earth. With us, through the ages, the populations of Galveston Island animals have faced the furious winds and all the other challenges of nature, going toe to toe with the elements. And yes, like us, they have survived.

How ironic it is that the force that will exterminate (and has) some of these wonderful Galveston populations is the very species that has fought to keep a toehold in this barren waste-land–man. It seems inevitable that our tiny fellow creatures, fighting the good fight with us, will succumb to the wrath of our very existence. We sap the freshwater, obliterate the forests, fill the saltwater with life-killing sediments, crush the beaches and road-crossers with our vehicle's tires, fill the air with pesticides and loose on the survivors animals as destructive as feral cats.

Make no mistake about it–Galveston Island is one of the most damaged ecosystems in the entire North American continent. The majority of reptile species are gone or virtually so; amphibians are down to a precious few; and many wild mammals are on the brink of disappearing. Nesting birds like skimmers are being harassed by people on ATVs and 4-wheelers, who seem to play egg-crushing contests between onslaughts on pristine dunes. Natural land areas are disappearing as fast as you can say, "Grease an official's palm," and lawless people destroying what little we have left make jokes about environmentalists.

Is there any hope? For far too many species, the answer is clearly "no." But it's not all gone. Not yet. The State Park and the Preserve are safe for now, but in the absence of prescribed burning, it will ecologically stray farther and farther from its natural course. As the neighborhood around the Preserve encroaches closer and closer, with construction noise and neighborhood cats, its effectiveness as a sanctuary lessens.

Developers defy the law and destroy isolated natural areas without permits, because the law–and those who enforce it–

San Luis Pass

have no teeth. On almost any warm weekend, vehicles destroy dunes on the west end of the island all day, and neither the police, sheriff or Texas Parks and Wildlife care about these priceless structures to patrol on more than very rare occasions. When the owners of this pristine ecosystem attempted to keep marauding vehicles out, they were nearly put in jail by the General Land Office. Is there an environmental conscience in the State of Texas?

Clearly, the maligned creatures of Galveston have only one hope for a champion. There must be an attitude change at the grassroots level. We must find it unacceptable to trade our kid's natural heritage for a few more bucks. We must replace greasy palms and fists full of dollars with helping hands for creatures perilously perched on the brink of oblivion. The average Galvestonian has to look beyond the bleakness of his or her checkbook and feel for helpless animals that have no place to go, no tree to nest in, no marsh to drink from, and no hope for tomorrow. If we really are a compassionate species, and somehow higher than these other creatures, let us join in a just cause to rescue our nonhuman neighbors from a fate that would be our worst nightmare.

From my perspective, above and beyond an attitude overhaul, these things need to happen:

1) The public must demand that all environmental laws be adhered to, in order to preserve the remaining vestiges of our natural areas.

2) Groups professing to care about the environment must stop feuding and work cooperatively to identify areas that need protecting, and devise plans to bring about said protection.

3) Our schools need to instill pride in their students about the unique ecosystem on which we live and educate them as to how to preserve its nature.

4) The media must adopt a "tell it like it is" philosophy about environmental destruction and be more informative about the natural resources we have.

104

5) Government agencies entrusted with environmental protection must take a hard line against illegal activities and sweet deals designed to give developers carte blanche.

6) Developers need to seek out professionals to help them plan sites to voluntarily reduce impact on wild animal populations.

7) Biologists should explore and monitor Galveston closely to ascertain exactly what is here and what populations need the greatest protection.

There are some positive steps being taken. Salt marsh preservation has become a serious task in very recent years. As we go to press, a large portion of worthless land along the I-45 corridor is being transformed into a new salt marsh and with time should become home to Clapper Rails, fiddler Crabs and Seaside Sparrows. This process is also being discussed for the bay side of the State Park, where acres of salt marsh have been lost to subsidence and other forces. Indeed, there seems to be positive gains in salt marsh acreage in the future.

One of Galveston's Salt Marshes

Another positive is the acquisition of forest patches by private individuals, or other entities that appear willing to protect them. Aside from the forest I bought and live in, Mary Alice O'Conell, an outstanding local birder, purchased a nice stretch of oaks by Eckert's Bayou to preserve. Another doctor and avid birdlister, Dwight Peake, owns some lovely acreage with oaks and fruiting trees in Spanish Grant.

Lawrence's Hammock near Eckert's Bayou

Army Corps Engineering forest

Aside from the sanctuary formally known as the Laffite's Cove Nature Preserve, there is a nice stretch of forest on U. S. Army land just off Ferry Road that seems destined for preservation. It is a low, dry forest which contains many herps and mammals, as well as birds.

Three forests I know of deserve some attention by conservation-minded people. One is the tiny patch of oaks and fruiting trees across the road, east of the Country Club Golf Course near the end of Stewart Road. Owned for years by Dr. Abe Levy (see Chapter 1), the fruiting trees in back are a bounty for songbirds in the spring. This land could easily be sold with disastrous results.

The second is the oaks adjacent to Dr. O'Connell's land on the east side of Eckert's Bayou. My only Lawrence's Warbler *ever* came from this place, and these two properties together make an excellent haven for spring and fall migrants.

The third is at the north end of 61st Street, on the left side of the dead end. This unique parcel is loaded with mulberries, figs, sugarberries and other treats for the birds, and seems to be owned by the automobile establishment across the street. What a place for a birder to put a small house!

Alhough not technically part of Galveston, the open forest at the end of the Pelican Island road is loaded with migrant birds and resident creatures, including nesting Painted Buntings. If anyone out there had the means to purchase any of these plots, the positive impact it would have on wildlife is incalculable.

But most folks (especially in Galveston) don't have this kind of "means." That doesn't mean they cannot help the struggle to save our natural resources. We all vote; we can all make phone calls, write letters, or go see officials to voice support for the environment. In the Clinton-Bush election of 1992, an exit poll revealed that less than **one percent (1%)** of the voters listed the environment as their chief issue. No wonder so many decisions go against our fellow earthlings!

Beaches are another critical ecosystem to birds, and, thanks to the Texas Open Beaches Act, they have enough beach traffic to constantly disturb birds. Most of these–gulls, terns, pelicans and many others–are carnivores. They need places to digest their huge meals and constantly having to fly creates an unhealthy situation for them. Many just leave the area.

Others such as plovers and sandpipers rely on the beach for their food, though it is still "meat." Plovers pick up invertebrates off the sand, and sandpipers probe just under the substrate for the worms that constitute their diet. In either event, studies have shown that automobiles crush the tiny food items (does anyone feel sorry for *them*?) which deprive shorebirds of their meals. Many of these plovers and sandpipers are on a north/south migration, where there is only *one* shore running parallel to their flight on which to feed. Protecting a portion of the beach at Apfell Park was a good start, but more needs to be set aside.

More and more, there are people who would prefer *some* beaches where cars are not allowed. They are certainly safer for small children, the shelling is excellent, and there are far fewer disturbances. People can fish, walk, beachcomb, sunbathe and goof around all they want to, without trucks and ATVs constantly whizzing by. Does it make too much sense to have *some* places for beach traffic and some without (other than a few private neighborhoods)?

Another habitat that deserves some protection is that of native grassland. Galveston Island is a reflection of the fact that, historically, there were millions of acres of this wonderful community, and now it (and its prairie chickens) has almost vanished. It was the dominant ecosystem here on the island in precolonial years, but now is confined to the State Park and a few isolated areas such as Indian Beach. Topping the list of enemies is the fact that they are sustained by fire, and fires are illegal within the city limits of Galveston–which is virtually the entire island.

Fire eliminates invasive, competitive plant and fungal species; it opens the ground for new growth, nutrients tied up in dead litter are recycled, and some plant species native to fire-tolerant communities cannot even reproduce in the absence of fire.

The State Park now manages the grassland with mowers, as does Indian Beach, which imitates fire only in small ways. It would be a great boost for Galveston ecology to have a properly maintained grassland, but that will take some legal maneuvering. I tried to gain a permit from the Fire Department for a portion of my property, and, despite having "done my homework," my application and appeal were summarily denied. But the illegal fires continue every weekend on the beach at San Luis Pass, despite the protests of the owner.

Sometimes it seems we have a long way to go. But I believe that if Galveston's conservation groups pull together, stand up for the natural areas and their inhabitants, and educate people– especially children–as to what we have here, there is hope. It is a new millennium, and the losses of the past century are irretrievable.

The ability of us survivors on this grand hunk of hurricane-pounded sand to create and/or save something of its wealth for future generations reminds me of the old story about the boy who tried to play a trick on his grandfather. He caught a wren in the garage and held it between his hands as he entered the house. Approaching his grandfather, he said, "I have a bird in my hands. Is it alive, or is it dead?" The boy had planned to release it unharmed if his grandfather said it was dead, and squeeze it to death if the answer was "alive." But being the wise old man that he was, and knowing the trick, Grand Dad simply said, "Son, the fate of that bird is in your hands."

And to you, the reader, the fate of this island is in your hands. Get involved.

Index